DAILY
WORD
for
TEENS

DISCOVERING
WHAT'S SACRED IN YOU

Written and edited by
Colleen Zuck, Elaine Meyer, and Laurie Daven

Printed in the United States of America
Rodale Inc. makes every effort to use acid-free ∞, recycled paper ♲.

Cover Designer: Joanna Williams
Cover and Interior Illustrator: Laurie Daven

"Prayer for a Journey" on page 230 used with permission, *Journey through Heartsongs* by Matthew James Thaddeus Stepanek © 2001.

Library of Congress Cataloging-in-Publication Data
Zuck, Colleen.
    Daily word for teens : discovering what's sacred in you / written and edited by Colleen Zuck, Elaine Meyer, and Laurie Daven
      p. cm.
    ISBN 1–57954–504–1 hardcover
    1. Teenagers—Prayer-books and devotions—English.
2. Devotional calendars—Unity School of Christianity.
I. Meyer, Elaine. II. Daven, Laurie. III. Title.
BV4850.Z83 2002
242'.63—dc21   2002069675

Distributed to the book trade by St. Martin's Press

2 4 6 8 10 9 7 5 3 1 hardcover

Visit us on the Web at www.rodalestore.com, or call us toll-free at (800) 848-4735.

WE **INSPIRE** AND **ENABLE** PEOPLE TO IMPROVE
THEIR LIVES AND THE WORLD AROUND THEM

An Invitation

Daily Word is the magazine of Silent Unity, a worldwide prayer ministry now in its second century of service. Silent Unity believes that:

- *All people are sacred*
- *God is present in all situations*
- *Everyone is worthy of love, peace, health, and prosperity*

Supported by free-will offerings, Silent Unity prays with all who ask for prayer. Every prayer request is held in absolute confidence. You are invited to contact Silent Unity 24 hours a day, any day of the year.

Write: Silent Unity, 1901 NW Blue Parkway
Unity Village, MO 64065-0001
Or call: (816) 969-2000   Fax: (816) 251-3554
Online: www.unityworldhq.org

There's More!

If you enjoy these inspirational messages, you may wish to subscribe to *Daily Word* magazine and receive a fresh, contemporary, uplifting message for each day of the month. With its inclusive, universal language, this pocket-size magazine is a friend to millions of people around the world.

For a free sample copy or for subscription information regarding *Daily Word* in English (regular and large-type editions) or in Spanish, please write:

Silent Unity, 1901 NW Blue Parkway
Unity Village, MO 64065-0001
Or call: (800) 669-0282   Fax: (816) 251-3554
Online: www.unityworldhq.org

Articles & Poems

INTRODUCTION

I magine for a few moments that you are going on a journey that might last several years. You will want to pack light but be sure you have what you need. You will probably include comfortable clothes for all kinds of weather and conditions. Don't forget important tools such as a map and even a compass so you won't spend a lot of time being lost.

You need wisdom, faith, and courage that will support you as you go into unfamiliar, unexplored territory. Meeting new people, being exposed to a diversity of ideas, and discovering your strengths along the way, you will never be bored. Leaving behind familiar people and places, you will rely on your core beliefs to get you through some challenges. You will learn from others and your own experiences and also teach others by your example.

You might or might not be surprised to know that as a teen, you are already on such a journey. You are no longer a child and not quite an adult. Yet during the next few years, you are without question on a journey of discovery. You will be or might already be asking yourself questions such as "Who am I—really?" And, "How do I fit in and what am I contributing to the world around me?"

We hope this book will be a helpful tool that you use often. Reading it, you will understand that you never have to go through anything alone; God is always with you and ready to help you make it through your greatest challenges and your most fulfilling accomplishments.

In page after page, you will be encouraged to know your true identity as a sacred being, created by God and capable of great and marvelous things. You are a member of the family of God, but like all of God's creations, you are unique. This means that no one else is exactly like you, and you are like no one else. No one else can take on the role that has been given to you. No one else can live your life for you, although it might seem as if people are trying to at times. Ultimately, you are responsible for being that wonderful creation that God created you to be.

"Teen" may be only one of many labels that people use to describe you. Yet you are first and foremost a spiritual being, for you were created in the image of God. That image is the invisible but all-powerful spirit of God that is always within you, ready to guide you.

We believe that between the covers of this book, you'll find practical, powerful tools to help you on your journey of discovering and living from the sacredness within you:

Daily messages: On each one you will find a quote, an affirmation, and a practical truth that you can apply to everyday life. Themes vary. Some examples are health, relationships, faith, and guidance.

Meditation pages: Using these guided meditations, you will learn to become still inside and get in touch with God's presence within you.

Journal pages: Each one will offer you a thought-provoking statement or question to jump-start you in writing down your thoughts and observations. Writing and then reading what you wrote will help you know yourself better and realize your strengths.

Stories: Here are true-life accounts by teens or by adults about their teen years. Subjects range from coping with a big family to overcoming self-destructive habits.

Creative pages: These poems and exercises will add enjoyment to your journey of discovery.

Why read this book? At the very least, you will get to know yourself better and have a closer relationship with God. We believe that as you take the messages, stories, and meditations into your heart and your life, you will treat yourself and others with reverence, love, and appreciation. You will recognize yourself and all others—regardless of age—as children of God. You will be encouraged to live as the sacred being that, in truth, you are.

—THE EDITORS

Looking Beyond a Label

By Marc

My name is Marc and I have dyslexia. Some think that it would be a disability, but to me it's a mere annoyance.

Let me explain my dyslexia. It's not like on television where the letters and numbers appear backwards to someone who is dyslexic. I can read most anything, as long as I have seen and memorized all of the words. I am unable to sound out words, and please don't ask me to spell anything.

Cursive writing looks like Greek to me. It's as if there are short circuits in my head that make it almost impossible for me to regurgitate information. Even words that I have used thousands of times look foreign when I put pen to paper. I know it's wrong as I'm writing it, but I can't tell just what is wrong. It's very hard just to organize my thoughts to write school papers or a simple note to my mom. Fortunately, Mom and Dad have become pretty good at deciphering what I have written, and the spell check is a lifesaver.

I encounter a lot of prejudice because of my spelling. People, including some teachers, think I'm stupid because of it. When I'm called on in class to give an answer, I can't always come up with the words that I really want to say, but I've been assured that this happens to lots of people—not just me.

When I was four, I was tested by the school system,

1

which decided my only problem was Attention Deficit Hyperactivity Disorder (ADHD). I was placed in Special Ed in the Behavior Disorder section. Let me tell you that—at least in this school system—you never want to be dumped in the BD program. In those classes you're treated as if your IQ is on the same level as a radish.

My education was spotty at best. A large portion of my day was spent in behavior modification meetings with counselors, and lots of "touchy-feely" things. The quality of my schoolwork was second to whether I was sitting in my seat as I was doing it. Fortunately, my parents fought to get me mainstreamed and worked with me at home to make sure I never lost my love of learning. They would never allow me to use ADHD or dyslexia as an excuse not to accomplish something. They've taught me that I am more than any label someone may try to put on me. Now museums are a second home to me. I've been to many operas, plays, and even one ballet.

My family and friends are great, too. They never treat me any differently than anyone else. Most important is my love for God. He's shown me that there is nothing I can't overcome and that any of the troubles I have are certainly small compared to the misfortunes of others. My mantra is "with God all things are possible." I believe in God and I believe in myself, and prayer has become a regular part of my daily routine. Like any other routine, it took time to become a habit, but now I do it regularly. I brush my teeth to clean them, I do my homework to stay ahead in class, and I say my prayers to God to keep my faith fresh and active.

I may not be able to change the attitudes of people who

judge me and put labels on me, but I can choose not to let what they say or do bother me. And I don't let it. With hard work and faith in God and myself, I've gotten my grades up and shown those who doubted me that I am capable of being more.

I'm now in high school and going to regular classes. I love working with computers and am currently taking a great class on computer repair and building, which comes naturally for me. If all goes well this year, I will be taking a test to be a certified computer technician. I've also been nominated by my teachers to participate in the People to People Student Ambassador program. Only a few students are chosen from each state once a year to travel to Australia for two months during the summer. If I'm accepted, I'll be learning about another culture, meeting members of the Parliament of Australia, and swimming in the Great Barrier Reef—all while getting school credit!

Sure, I still have problems in school with essay tests and writing assignments, but if that's the hardest thing I have to face in my life, then I guess I'm not doing too badly.

Prayer
for Protection

BY JAMES DILLET FREEMAN

The light of God surrounds us;
The love of God enfolds us;
The power of God protects us;
The presence of God watches over us.
Wherever we are, God is!

New Start

---◆---

"We are all capable of change and growth;
we just need to know where to begin."
—Blaine Lee

Change can be a painful experience. When a relationship ends or changes, when my family moves to a new neighborhood, or when a job doesn't work out, I may feel like I have to start all over again.

Starting again is easier when I remember that through all the changes, God is the one constant in my life. God is right here inside me and everywhere around me. God knows me, loves me, and supports me through every change.

So anytime I am making a new start, I know the right words to say and the right steps to take. I remember that God is here with me and within me, and my words and actions come naturally.

I know I have the courage to pick myself up and try again, whatever the circumstances. When I connect with God's presence within me, I realize God is here to give me the love, courage, and support I need to start again.

God supports me through every change
and every new start.

DISCOVERY

—◆—

"You can't get there by bus, only by hard work and risk and by not quite knowing what you're doing. What you'll discover will be wonderful. What you'll discover will be yourself."
—Alan Alda

Sometimes I might wonder if I have what it takes to make it in life. I might feel a twinge of doubt in the back of my mind that slowly finds its way to the surface of my thoughts. But then I hand these concerns over to God in prayer, and I am completely at peace.

Any doubt that I might have had is quickly replaced with confidence and a surge of excitement as God assures me that I will never go through any challenge alone. God will show me where I need to go and what I need to do. With God, I discover a new way and a new, self-confident me. I discover that all it takes is the power of the Almighty One to show me that I can be more.

I am not traveling through life alone. The Almighty One is supporting and guiding me as I explore life's possibilities. With God, I have the wisdom and strength to discover a whole new world.

*Each day I discover more about myself
and what God can accomplish through me.*

Daily Word for Teens

HOLY GROUND

◆

*"The Lord said to him, 'Take off the sandals from your feet,
for the place where you are standing is holy ground.'"*
—Acts 7:33

I don't have to be in a recognized place of worship to
be on holy ground. In the cafeteria at school, in my room
at home, in my favorite spot outdoors, in a store, or even
at the dentist's office—wherever I am, I bring holiness to
that place. Why? Because I am a temple of God's spirit.
God resides within my body and soul. So wherever I am
is holy.

God's presence is everywhere. So as I journey through
life, I know that with each step I take, I am walking on
holy ground. I might feel tempted to rush into the future,
or I might wish I was living in a different place, but I
know that right now, right here, is exactly where I am
supposed to be.

Instead of impatiently pushing for changes to happen
in my life, I let God's plan for my future unfold naturally,
present moment by present moment. I begin to see the
sacredness in everything I am going through now and in
the lessons I am learning.

*Right now, right here, I am exactly where
I am meant to be. I am on holy ground.*

PARENTS

—◆—

*"It is very difficult to live among people you love
and hold back from offering them advice."*
—Anne Tyler

There is one thing my parents seem to be ready to give plenty of, and that's advice. They give it, of course, because they love and care about me. I remember this when my parents are telling me what to do. Silently I say, "It's because you love me."

I am learning from my parents: what to do and what not to do if and when I choose to be a parent—just as they must have learned from their own parents. I understand that my peaceful, positive attitude can help my parents be better parents.

I know that my parents and I want to be even more loving to one another. Just by imagining in prayer that God's love is flowing between us, I am encouraging that flow of love to increase. We are loving more and learning more each day how to be the best mother, father, daughter, or son we can be. My prayer is that my parents and I express more and more of God's love to one another.

*I give thanks for the love that is flowing
between my parents and me.*

MUSIC FOR MY SOUL

◆

*"I was born with music inside me . . . Music was one of my parts . . .
Like my blood. It was a force already within me when I arrived
on the scene. It was a necessity for me—like food or water."
—Ray Charles*

The pulsating rhythm of the bass playing on the radio
or the uplifting lyrics of a song seem to charge me with
energy. I feel joy lifting me up as I sing out loud, and I
do—even off-key—because it makes me happy. The
music that stirs my soul may not be the same kind of
music that speaks to others, and that's okay. What is
important is that I listen to what speaks to my soul.

God's music—the sounds of creation—speaks to my
soul and fills me with joy, too. The laughter of my friends
is music to my ears, and so is the sound of birds singing
or crickets chirping. These are sounds that remind me of
the sacredness of life that is all around me. Listening, I
can feel that I am one with all creation.

Music for my soul to enjoy surrounds me—whether it
is flowing from nature or from my favorite CD—and I
take time to listen to it and enjoy it.

*I listen to the sounds that speak
to my soul and fill me with joy.*

CAR BLESSING

—◆—

"My presence will go with you."
—Exodus 33:14

As my friends and I learn to drive a car, I am discovering a new appreciation for transportation. I feel a newfound sense of freedom. With that freedom comes the responsibility to observe the rules of the road. I am committed to being a careful and considerate driver.

Because I am also committed to a spiritual way of life, I add a higher dimension to my thoughtfulness as a driver. Before I take the wheel, I fasten my seatbelt. I imagine God's order working as a spirit of cooperation through me and through each driver on the road. In my mind I picture the traffic flowing in an orderly way at every intersection, at every highway entrance and exit. As I travel, I bless my car and every car, driver, and passenger with a prayer for safety:

"God, You are in charge. I see divine order at work because You are continually guiding us on safe roads to our destinations."

God's order is working as a spirit of cooperation
through me and through each driver on the road.

MEDITATION
I Am Unique

◆

Sitting quietly in a comfortable position, I breathe deeply and begin to relax. I feel relaxation spreading from my head down to my toes. As I think of my body, I marvel that nowhere on Earth is there anyone with exactly these same dancing eyes, loving arms, and serving hands.

Completely relaxed, I turn my attention to the inner qualities that make me special and different. The way I laugh, the things that are important to me, my dreams for the future—all are ways that I fill a special place in the world.

Returning from this quiet place in my mind, I feel appreciation for my uniqueness. I don't need to be like anyone else. I do need to be *me*, because no one else can do that but me. I am growing into my full expression as a priceless God original. And as I express God's love in all I do, I am being the wonderful me that God has designed me to be.

*I fill a special place in the world as
a unique expression of God's love.*

TOO FUNNY!

I still laugh when I think of certain memories.
I remember when:

_____

_____

_____

_____

_____

_____

_____

_____

_____

_____

_____

_____

CAPTURE THE MOMENT

—◆—

"You don't take a photograph, you make it."
—Ansel Adams

Using a camcorder or camera, I can capture a moment in time and then enjoy looking at it again later. I also use my mind to capture personal memories—ones that are purely my own, from my own recollection. When I am alone, I reflect on some of these memories.

I may have memories of difficult times that were painful, but they are only memories and no longer have the power to hurt me. I can now look back on those times and see that whether or not I was aware of it, God was with me, bringing me through.

I have also stored special moments when I felt the joy of just being alive. I remember fun times that I shared with people who truly cared about me. So whenever I'm feeling down, I replay those good times and relive the joy that I felt back then.

I give thanks for my mind, for it is a wonderful tool that enables me to capture special moments in time.

I capture special moments as memories
that can be replayed and enjoyed all over again.

Daily Word for Teens

TRUSTWORTHY

"These words are mine and they are true."
—Chief Meninock

It is exciting to watch a trapeze artist take a leap of faith into midair and grasp the arms of a partner at just the right moment. To feel safe in taking such a risk, they must have a high level of trust in each other. Both acrobats must be sure to be right where they said they would be and at just the right moment. Their lives actually depend on each other's trustworthiness.

I try always to be that kind of person. If I say, "I will be there," it is true. I don't let my friends and family members down by casually changing my mind at the last minute. If I say, "I won't tell," I keep my lips zipped. If I say, "I will stand by you," then I *am* there for them when they need me most. If something does happen that prevents me from keeping a commitment, I communicate to explain and to ask if there is another way I can "be there" and give my support. I am trustworthy!

Others trust me, and I trust myself,
because I keep my word.

KUDOS!

*"Treasure what is unique and internal and valuable
in yourself and your own personal evolution."*
— Jean Shinoda Bolen, M.D.

Sometimes the pressures to succeed in school, work,
and sports can be overwhelming. It's rewarding to be
congratulated for accomplishing great things, but
sometimes it feels good to give myself a round of "kudos"
just for being me.

I may not be the captain of the team or the head of
the class, but that's okay—I don't put myself down or
compare myself to others. I value myself for working on
and accomplishing the things that are important to me.
Maybe I have overcome a physical challenge, said "no"
to friends who were pressuring me to do something
unwise, released an unhealthy habit, or healed a hurt in
a relationship with someone. I am accomplishing great
things that are helping me build integrity and strength of
character.

I give thanks to God for the things I have accomplished
in my life already, and for the successes yet to come. And
I congratulate myself for being me.

*I value and respect myself for accomplishing
the goals that are important to me.*

EXPECT A MIRACLE

◆

*"God added his testimony by signs and wonders
and various miracles."*
—Hebrews 2:4

Miracles do happen, even when I'm not aware of them. In fact, I expect them to happen as a natural part of God's plan. If what I am praying for seems impossible, then I am not really having faith in the outcome. But when I pray *knowing* that God is answering my prayer, I am expecting good to happen. My attitude shifts from hopelessness to "everything is working out for good!" Now that's real faith!

I pray with complete trust in God, turning the need over to God to answer my prayer in the best way possible. I don't yet see all the possibilities, but God does. I don't limit my possibilities by stubbornly thinking that only I know the best answer to my prayer! But I do stubbornly refuse to see anything but good happening in the situation I am praying about. I know God has it covered.

I ask in prayer, and I expect miracles as a natural response from God, because miracles do happen!

*I gratefully expect and receive miracles
as a natural part of God's plan.*

Daily Word for Teens

Being in Love

*"We come to love not by finding a perfect person,
but by learning to see an imperfect person perfectly."*
—Sam Keen

Being in love can seem like the greatest feeling in the world! It's true that God's love is within me all the time, but when I am "in love," I choose to open my heart to that one certain person. As I do, I feel God's love within me even more.

Being in love can also seem like the worst feeling in the world. If I find myself going through a breakup, I might feel sad and rejected. It feels as if the love has gone away along with that special someone. I might close my heart to try to protect myself. And the secret is, that's when it really hurts! When I become angry, sad, or afraid, I prevent myself from feeling God's love, even though it is always there.

The love I was feeling didn't come from the other person, but from opening my heart to God's love within and all around me. So I realize that just by opening my heart and seeing the perfection in everything, I can be "in love" with life all the time!

*I keep my heart open to the love of God
that is within me and all around me.*

CREATIVE

—◆—

*"Somewhere, something incredible
is waiting to be known."*
—Carl Sagan

Taking a lesson from the penguin—a bird that can no longer fly—I am determined not to lose my ability to be creative. The saying "Use it or lose it" encourages me to be creative.

Just for fun, I think of myself exercising the muscles of my brain regularly. I use them so that I won't lose them. I actually strengthen my creative muscles as I practice the ways I can be creative:

I have a style—a distinctive way of looking and acting and speaking that gives expression to me. That takes creativity and maybe some courage at times, because I may step outside the box of what's "in." My talents may be expressed as an artistic flair or academic skills, as a totally compassionate nature or an analytical mind-set.

The more I practice expressing myself, the more confidence I feel in taking the risk to share my original ideas with others. I am creative!

*I have an incredible ability to be creative
that is strengthened each time I use it.*

MEDITATION
Circle of Love

◆

In a special place where I can be alone with my thoughts, I close my eyes and get comfortable. With music playing softly, I go within to the sacred center of my being where the spirit of God greets me.

My focus is on God and the unlimited love that my Creator is pouring out to me. I take a deep breath, and as I release it, I feel the warm glow of love filling my body. God loves me unconditionally.

My physical body seems to be asleep, but my mind has never before been so awake. I see myself at the very center of a circle of love, surrounded by family, friends, and others. God's love is expressing through them as compassion and understanding.

I move toward the outline of people who make up the circle, and I become a part of it. I am now expressing pure love to all. This is how it feels to be loved and to love. I thank God, for now that I know, I will always be open to receiving and giving love.

*I both receive and give love
in a circle of love.*

HELP FOR THE PLANET

I can do so many things to help
the environment. Some ideas are:

_____

_____

_____

_____

_____

_____

_____

_____

_____

_____

_____

_____

Inspiring Others

By Leanne

W hen my advisor at my high school in Hawaii showed me pictures of nearby Kualoa beach, a public beach that was littered with trash, he said, "Somebody has got to do something about this!" Since I was the president of the One World Club, an environmental club at my school, he asked, "Will you go ahead and try to do something right away?"

I had gotten interested in the environment when I attended a lecture by Brian Schatz, the creator of YES, the Youth for Environmental Services program. Up until that time, I had thought working on environmental projects would involve being around a lot of bugs and getting really dirty.

I liked working with people, and then I began to think about how important my environment of beautiful mountains, trees, and parks had been to me. I realized that there were a lot of things that were going wrong in my familiar environment. That's when I decided to take a leadership role and do something to help make things right.

As president of the One World Club, I juggled my high school activities and homework with my work for the environment. Sometimes I would work on a project all night, and other times I spent five minutes to an hour here or there. I did whatever I could do.

I asked my friends to help with my first beach cleanup, but they said, "Oh, it's just another beach cleanup. There's really nothing to it." They didn't support me, so I did it all by myself. The second and third time, they were like, "Oh, we've got to help!" It was really kind of funny to see how quickly their attitudes changed.

They helped me a lot with the community service projects, and we always had a lot of fun, because we enjoyed just being together, playing but getting the work done!

The cleanup of Kualoa, a favorite place to camp or jog for many people, would be a big project. I contacted government officials and complained, "What's going on at Kualoa beach? Why isn't someone picking up the old fish nets and other trash that's littering the beach?" The answer they gave me was incredible: "There are no fish nets or trash there!"

So finally I just said, "Okay, why don't I just go ahead and organize a cleanup?" I did a mass mailing and called a whole bunch of people. My friends were eager to help. All of a sudden I had about sixty volunteers—so many I didn't know what to do with them!

What we found during the cleanup was amazing: five or six huge fish nets all tangled into one huge mess, old buoys, fish parts, and other litter. After the cleanup, the beach looked like the Hawaiian beauty it truly was.

The Kualoa cleanup was a perfect example of people seeing something wrong—something worth complaining about—and then instead of continuing to complain, actually doing something about it.

Recently, I have been participating in a program called Hooulu, which means "inspire." We bring together younger students with older students who are active in the community. The older students show the younger ones that just because we are kids doesn't mean we can't do something. In fact, we all can.

This is true: It only takes one person to inspire everyone else. That one person may not be all that organized starting out or may not have a perfect plan, but by doing something really worth doing, things will get better. I know from my own experiences that that's absolutely right.

MY WALK WITH GOD

—◆—

"Even though I walk through the darkest valley,
I fear no evil; for you are with me."
—Psalms 23:4

If I could see the trail of my footsteps over the last year or two, I might see places where I walked with determination and purpose. At other times, I suddenly turned back and changed direction. Maybe one of the times I turned back was when I walked away from a car when I was not sure that the person driving was a capable, responsible driver. I was divinely guided not to do something that would put my life in jeopardy.

The truth is that God is always walking with me, ready to guide me. It's up to me to be aware of God and to follow divine guidance. Sometimes I may want to do something so much that I talk myself into doing it even though it just doesn't feel right. Then I know that I am taking a detour from my walk with God.

The good news is that I can change my mind and change my direction, and I do. Prayer and meditation reawaken my God awareness, and I move in the right direction.

God is always walking with me, ready to guide me.

Daily Word for Teens

I'M A STAR!

—◆—

"Beauty comes in all ages, colors, shapes, and forms.
God never makes junk."
—Kathy Ireland

How often have I watched a celebrity on TV or in a movie and fantasized about how great it would feel to be idolized by thousands? Well, even if I never achieve such stardom, I know that I am a star in my own right. I am outstanding and magnificent because I give expression to the glory of God in whatever I do and say.

Even if my name never appears in lights, I am still a star! What I do in life validates who I am, so I always try to do my best and give one-hundred percent in all that I do—even if it's something as tedious as homework or a part-time job. I serve as a shining example to others. There is a confidence in my walk and a conviction in my words.

I don't need to take center stage and have the admiration of others to feel good about myself. I am a star that shines brightly because I glow with the life and love of God.

With God's love to support me,
I am successful in whatever I do.

Daily Word for Teens

NOTHING TO FEAR

—◆—

"All we need to do is expose fears
to the sunlight and they shrink."
—Dale Dauten

I am learning to see the world in a whole new way:
I know that God is everywhere present. That means
that whether I am walking at night or in the light of day,
whether I am in an unfamiliar or a familiar place, or
whether I am doing something new or something I have
practiced many times, God is with me. Just like darkness
is the absence of light, fear is just the absence of love.
And since God's love is right here within my very own
heart, I am protected. I simply shine the light of love on
every situation, every person, every new challenge—and
the fear disappears.

For instance, if I am afraid of making a mistake in front
of a group or an audience, I remember to send them love
as I speak or perform. They will receive my message of
love and mirror it right back to me! If I am feeling scared
in a new environment, I imagine God's love, like a
floodlight, dispelling the darkness. In the bright light of
love, I see that there is nothing to fear.

The light of God surrounds me and protects me
wherever I am.

Daily Word for Teens

INNER BEAUTY

—◆—

*"Let your adornment be the inner self
with the lasting beauty of a gentle and quiet spirit,
which is very precious in God's sight."
—1 Peter 3:4*

I don't always notice my true beauty when I look into a mirror. So I put aside the mirror and the reflection that might have revealed what I think of as imperfections. Then I take another look at myself—a look within—and this is what I see:

There is a light of incredible beauty that is always shining inside me. This is a beauty of spirit, God's spirit, that I let shine out as life and wisdom, love and enthusiasm. The beauty of spirit sparkles in everything I say and do. It conveys warmth that draws others to me and allows them to feel comfortable whenever they are with me.

A sacred, inner beauty radiates from the holy presence within me, the presence of God. As I let it shine, I encourage others to let their inner light shine, too. What a powerful glow of light and love we create together as, person by person, we add to the beauty of our world.

*The beauty of God's spirit within me
shines out into my world.*

GUIDANCE

—◆—

"In the book of life, the answers aren't in the back."
—*Charlie Brown*

Every day I am learning more—even when I am not in school—because the world is my classroom and God is my teacher.

I receive guidance in prayer when I let go of my own ideas about how things should turn out. I trust God to lead me, and I listen for the answers that come as an inner knowing or feeling in my heart.

I follow God's guidance to the opportunities that will bring me joy and fulfillment. I am led by God to the kinds of friends that will nurture and support me. God leads me with intuition that helps me to know the most loving things to say and do for others. God shows me when to offer my help, and when to trust that others will learn by helping themselves. God guides me in being the best person I can be and in seeing the best in others.

As my teacher, God is gently, lovingly guiding me to be the best "me" that I can be!

Thank You, God, for guiding me
and for caring about and for me.

Focus

*"Whatever is true, whatever is honorable, whatever is just,
whatever is pure, whatever is pleasing, whatever
is commendable . . . think about these things."*
—*Philippians 4:8*

Noticing the kinds of thoughts I've been having lately,
I realize that when I dwell on negative things, I feel
dissatisfied. But when I keep my attention focused on the
beauty and wonder of God, I see that there is good in
every person and in every moment.

Focusing on the good things in life, I look at everyone
and everything with appreciation for the divine wisdom
that was devoted to creating each one. I see the sunlight
sparkling on the morning dew that covers flowers and
grass. I watch stars twinkling far above me on a black
velvet sky. I see the good qualities in myself and other
people. Taking all of this in, I cannot help but appreciate
the divine power that created such beauty. I feel renewed
joy about life.

Because I focus my attention on the good, I see the
beauty in everyone and everything. My spirits are lifted as
I focus on the beauty and wonder of God everywhere.

*With my focus on God, I see for myself the beauty
of creation that surrounds me.*

29

Daily Word for Teens

MEDITATION
A Time of Prayer

◆

Like most people, I have a favorite spot at home—
a place where I can sit back, settle in, and let go of
anything that is bothering me. To fully let go, I take
time out for prayer and meditation.

When I close my eyes, I might still see flickers of
light that dance across the darkness, eventually fading
away. As I continue on with my eyes closed, I drift
deeper into that still, silent space.

Like welcoming friends, the darkness and silence
hug me. I listen, and God speaks to me in a language
of love and wisdom that my soul responds to with a
surge of joy.

In this sacred place, time no longer exists, and I
feel safe and secure. Here I can speak to God about
anything that's on my mind and heart. God listens
and understands my thoughts and feelings.

Returning from this quiet place, I am renewed and
ready to face this day with confidence.

*In my times of prayer, God listens to me
and understands me.*

SMILE!

How many times can I remember smiling today?
What was it about each time?

_____

_____

_____

_____

_____

_____

_____

_____

_____

_____

_____

_____

Daily Word for Teens

Having Fun

—◆—

"It's kind of fun to do the impossible."
—Walt Disney

I know how to have fun—especially when I am doing something that I really like to do. Yet, having some fun with *whatever* I am doing sure would make time go by more quickly and would make any kind of work a lot easier.

Fun makes any situation less stressful for me. Saying that I can have a good time cleaning my room may be stretching my fun theory a bit, but just maybe while I'm cleaning I listen to my favorite music and dance. That could be fun!

I can have fun being active—swimming or riding a roller coaster—but I can also have fun spending time being with or talking on the phone to my best friend, sharing my hopes and dreams.

Daydreaming is fun, because it gives me a chance to play with the imagination God gave me. Having fun can be worked into my day every day, and I choose to do just that.

I plan on discovering how much fun
I can include in whatever I do today.

JUST LIKE ME

—◆—

"I will give them one heart, and put a new spirit within them . . .
Then they shall be my people, and I will be their God."
—Ezekiel 11:19–20

When I am hanging out with my friends or in a crowd of strangers, do I stop to consider that we all have something sacred in common? We are creations of God.

All people are just like me in that we share a spiritual identity. I am thankful for the diversity within my home, school, neighborhood, and world; however, even though we may look and talk differently, we are all members of God's family.

Sometimes I might think that no one understands me, but I know that, just like me, the people in my immediate family and my group of friends are facing doubts and problems. We do our best when we support each other and believe that we are capable of great things because of what God can do through us.

I want to be loving, kind, and considerate and to remember that even though we have our differences, on the inside, everyone is just like me.

I have something in common with all people:
just like me, they are each a creation of God.

Meeting Challenges

---◆---

*"I have always grown from my problems
and challenges, from the things that don't work out.
That's when I've really learned."
—Carol Burnett*

When something unexpected happens in class or at home that has me feeling edgy or uncertain, there is something I can do to meet the challenge and even to beat it. I keep my thoughts God-centered, and I am able to do this by taking time out from the day to pray.

While I'm praying, I don't have to try to come up with the right answer or solution; I leave that to God. Instead, I pray with an attitude of gratitude that the blessings of God are happening at just the right time and in exactly the right way. God helps me meet any challenge by boosting my self-confidence. With such confidence, I keep my head held high.

Whatever is happening, I know that I will learn and grow from having relied on God. God always knows what is in my highest good, so I never go wrong when I trust God to help me through this day and every day.

God helps me meet every challenge.

EVERYTHING I NEED

◆

*"My teacher said to me, 'The treasure house within you
contains everything, and you are free to use it.
You don't need to seek outside.'"*
—Zen master Dazhu

I am not bragging when I say, "Everything I need to
know is within me or on its way to me," because I am not
just talking about myself. I am talking about my God-
given ability to think and reason. And even more than
that, I have intuition—an inner, sacred, instant knowledge
of the answers I need.

I know when something is right for me or if it's not.
What I do with that knowledge shapes my life every day.
At times, I may feel pressured to do more or be more, and
I may wonder if I can make it through the next few
months or years. At those times, I remember who I am: a
divine creation who has everything I need to be healthy,
happy, and free.

As God's creation, I am a living, breathing miracle of
life. I have abilities and talents that I have yet to discover
and explore. I do have everything I need, because God
has created me to live a full and satisfying life.

*I have everything I need to do whatever
my heart's desire leads me in doing.*

DANCE!

◆

"Dance like nobody's watching."
—Bono

I might not think of myself as a great dancer, and I might feel a little hesitant about dancing in front of anyone. But when the music starts, my body starts moving and I know I *want* to dance.

No matter what other forms of self-expression interest me, life asks me to "dance" my part, even if I am feeling nervous at first about being in the spotlight. Life asks that I participate fully in expressing myself in all the ways that call to me—and life asks that I not allow any self-doubt to limit me.

I am glad that there is a true and strong voice within my soul that reminds me: "I was born to dance my part in life as a completely capable, loveable, wonderful creation of God—and that is just what I am!" I can and do express myself boldly and confidently when I remember this truth. Holding to this thought, I come out of my shell, and I dance my part in life with joy!

*I participate boldly and confidently
in the dance of life!*

MY FAMILY

◆

*"Let us make one point, that we meet each other with a smile,
when it is difficult to smile. Smile at each other,
make time for each other in your family."*
—Mother Teresa

My family is a miracle of sorts! For eons of time,
people fell in love and married, had children and raised
them in order for the individuals of my family to be
together on planet Earth at this time.

Thinking of my family as the result of some divine
plan of life helps, because no matter the size of my
family, living in the same house and sharing space can be
a real challenge for me—and for them, too.

I smile when I think about how different in personality
and looks we may be, yet how alike we are, too. We each
need to be loved and to love. We each need to feel that
our home is a safe haven, a place where we not only
accept one another, but we also welcome one another
each time we come home.

The results of a united family are worth the effort it
takes, so I do my part. The respect and love I contribute
to my family go a long way in making things better for all
of us.

*The loving acceptance I give to my family
enriches them and also enriches me.*

Hopes and Dreams

◆

Closing my eyes as if to sleep, I let the cares of the day slip away. I relax my body, and I allow myself to be gently transported to that quiet place within where there is no one but God and me.

"God, You have created me with dreams for the future that are unique to me. My hopes and dreams reveal the purpose for which You have created me. I dare to imagine the things that really fill me with joy, knowing that You have given these dreams to me to lead me to my highest good. I am here to serve You, God. I allow my dreams of the future to lead me where You would have me go. I am open to Your plan for me, for I know that You have designed a life for me that is more fulfilling than I can imagine."

I linger here in this quiet place, as my hopes and dreams become clear. As I return my awareness to my body, I am refreshed with new hope for a bright today and a fulfilling future.

My hopes and dreams are revealing the mystery of my life's purpose to me.

PARENTS

I appreciate my parents because of
the things they do, such as:

_____

_____

_____

_____

_____

_____

I show them my appreciation by:

_____

_____

_____

_____

_____

_____

A New Life

By Richard

I was driving home one day when the man I blamed for ruining my life crossed the street in front of my car, a perfect target. I had savored the possibility of this moment. I would step on the gas, hear the roar of the engine, and flatten that sucker.

But in real life, when I finally had my chance, something had changed. As he hesitated in front of my car with a startled expression, I found myself smiling and waving hello. I had forgiven him.

My anger at this man began when we were both teenagers. Riding together in a car one hot summer day, he fell asleep at the wheel—and my world fell apart.

The accident happened so fast. Just after being thrown from the passenger seat, I was hit by the car as it rolled. Covered with blood and in extreme pain, my anxiety over how badly I had been hurt grew with each passing minute during the ambulance ride.

But when the ambulance stopped and the doors opened, I saw a familiar face waiting for me outside the hospital's emergency entrance. Love took visible form in my mother's face. She kissed my forehead. Although no words were spoken, I felt her assurance that everything would be okay.

Later, however, I learned that I was paralyzed from the waist down. I thought my life was over—at least the life I had known as captain of the basketball team and city high-jump champion. I lost all faith—in God and in myself—but my mother's faith never wavered. She continued to love me and pray for me even through my worst moments.

One of those moments came when my mother was exercising my legs. She would move my legs for me, doing what I could no longer do myself. Feeling such anger over my condition, I lashed out, yelling and thrashing my arms. After I had finished venting, Mom tapped my leg, and said, "Let's keep going."

The blame and hatred I was putting on the young man who had been driving continued to consume me. It was crippling me more than the paralysis.

One day, I picked up one of my mother's *Daily Word* magazines.The word for that day was forgiveness. It said that forgiveness doesn't let someone else off the hook. It frees us from the self-imposed hell of resentment and blame. Suddenly I understood that through forgiveness, I had the power to free myself from the hate that was ruining my life.

Forgiveness was the beginning of a new life for me. That new life has not been easy, but it is always meaningful. I am a professional speaker and ordained minister; driving, travelling by air, and walking with the aid of braces and crutches. I love and appreciate life now even more than I did before the accident.

This accident taught me more than forgiveness. It taught me faith, appreciation, and how to enjoy life even when it's not going my way. As Helen Keller said, "I thank God for my handicaps, for through them I have found myself, my work, and my God."

A Small Voice

By Emily

There's a little voice
In the depth of your mind
"Do this, not that"
You know the kind.

It says what's good,
It says what's bad.
It's almost a mini-version
Of lessons from Mom and Dad.

"Don't do drugs."
"Drive safe at night."
It almost seems nagging,
But it's usually right.

When you're put on the spot
And your friends are around
You do what they say,
Or you'll be put down.

That little voice
Speaks loud and clear:
"Don't listen to them!"
"Don't give into fear!"

Character is judged
By your little voice
It helps you pick friends
And make every choice.

ACCEPTANCE

◆

"Happiness can exist only in acceptance."
—Denis De Rougamont

I can accept that there will be times that friends and family and teachers do not agree with me about something that I feel passionate about. We can agree to disagree. I respect their viewpoints and I hope they respect mine.

I imagine myself saying, "I accept you as you are and for who you are." My attitude of acceptance reaches out to others. Although we may not think alike, speak the same language, or even dress similarly, each one of us is a unique creation of God.

Sometimes I really wish they wouldn't, but parents and teachers do make decisions that affect me. I could gripe about them and refuse to cooperate, but that would make the situation even harder to live with. So instead, I lighten up. When I stop resisting and start accepting circumstances that I can't change and that I might not have chosen for myself, I am amazed to find how much more peaceful I feel inside.

I am happy to be an accepting, understanding person.

Daily Word for Teens

The Light Within

—◆—

"Above the cloud with its shadow is the star with its light.
Above all things reverence thyself."
—Pythagoras

I am like a stained glass window—but others may not see how truly beautiful I am until they see God's light shining through me. The source of this light is God's spirit within me.

The light of God shines through me when I am with my friends, helping them out with a project. I glow with the enthusiasm I would feel if I were the one receiving the help.

I shine when I'm going into a new class for the first time, because the love of God is giving me the courage to smile and make the necessary small talk it takes to introduce myself and make new friends.

The light of God within me is a glow of faith that is visible to others. They can see it in my willingness to let my life unfold how it may, through my courage to take hold of life with enthusiasm, and my eagerness to live each moment to the fullest.

I am filled with the light of God.

The beauty of God's light shines from me
for all to see.

MY ROOM IS SACRED

—◆—

"Do my dreaming and my scheming; Lie awake and pray; Do my crying and my sighing; Laugh at yesterday . . . in my room."
—Brian Wilson (The Beach Boys)

There is one place on Earth that I claim as my very own: my room. Even if I share my room with a brother or sister, there is a part of that room that is just for me. I honor myself by making my room a clean and comfortable place to hang out on my own. In my room I can listen to music, take a nap, write in my journal, spend time in prayer, or tap into my imagination by daydreaming.

I can make my own sacred place in my room by creating my own altar. In a little corner spot, on a square of colorful cloth, I arrange objects that remind me of my connection to God: inspiring books, unusual seashells and rocks, and treasured photos of friends, family members, and pets. Anything that reminds me of my divinity and the sacredness of life can be a part of my altar. This is my special corner for praying and meditating, my own personal retreat where I am alone with God.

I create my room as a sacred place
for being by myself and for connecting with God.

POWER OF WORDS

—◆—

"Pleasant words are like a honeycomb,
sweetness to the soul and health to the body."
—Proverbs 16:24

I know how down I can feel when somebody says something cruel to me. Keeping that thought in mind, I try to choose my words carefully. How would I respond if I were on the receiving end of those words? Are they supportive? Are they loving? Would I feel comfortable saying them to God?

What I say and how I say it are important. Instead of reacting emotionally to what someone has said, I take a little time to make my words God-directed. Then I won't be kicking myself later for something I said in the heat of the moment.

If someone approaches me with a less-than-friendly attitude, I think thoughts of God before I speak. If I am introducing myself to someone I've never met before, my words echo a message of friendship.

My words have the power to impress and inspire, so I choose to speak words that convey the truth of God's presence within me.

I think thoughts of God before I speak,
because my words have power.

Daily Word for Teens

POSSIBILITIES

—◆—

"I am neither an optimist nor pessimist,
but a 'possibilist.'"
—Max Lerner

I get really excited when I am looking forward to doing certain things: shopping at the mall, learning to drive a car, swimming with my friends. When I picture myself in these scenes, I think of great possibilities and get ready for fun times.

The possibilities I imagine are like previews of coming attractions playing on the screen of my mind that prepare me to enjoy whatever is next. Things may not turn out exactly as I pictured them, but by expecting good, I am ready to see the good in whatever happens.

God gives me a vivid imagination to help me expect good. Somehow, expecting great possibilities helps me draw them to myself. My expectations make me a magnet for wonderful happenings. I am charged up and ready to accept the most in life, but I know that what God has prepared for me is even better than what I can imagine.

When I consider possibilities, I preview the good
that is coming to me.

TODAY

—◆—

*"Don't listen to those who say you're taking too big
a chance. Michelangelo would have painted the
Sistine floor, and it would surely be rubbed out by today."*
—Neil Simon

Instead of regretting things I did or didn't do, I remember that today is a gift to be experienced. Rather than always thinking about what I could, should, or would have done, I shrug off the regret and think of today as another opportunity. I know that I am doing the best I can each day.

Each new day is a new beginning—a chance to apply myself to improve the things I can in my life.

If things don't work out, that's okay. Failure is no longer a word that exists in my vocabulary. My world isn't going to come to an end just because I didn't succeed in a goal or complete a project this time—across the world it's already tomorrow, and I'll have many more tomorrows to try again!

I give myself a boost by firmly reminding myself: I have every reason to believe I will succeed today, because I am doing the best I can do to be the best me I can be!

*Today is a new opportunity,
and I gladly accept it.*

MEDITATION
Revelation

◆

When I want to receive inspiration from God, I find a quiet place to retreat. As I breathe deeply and relax, I let go of all the busy thoughts in my mind. The words and pictures that were crowding my mind simply fade away.

Now my mind is a blank canvas, and I am ready to receive a divine message that is meant especially for me. I remain still, not asking any questions, because God already knows what's on my heart and mind. I am simply resting in the comforting presence of God. I listen with a loving attitude, because God is revealing what I need to know. I experience this knowing as words I hear and emotions I feel, as beautiful symbols and pictures I see in my mind, or simply as a peaceful awareness I sense with my entire being.

I stay while God reveals the truth that my soul needs to hear. Then I return to my day with a renewed feeling of peace.

As I quiet my thoughts and become still, I receive revelations from God that tell me all I need to know.

HEALTHY EATING

—◆—

"You don't have to cook fancy or complicated masterpieces—
just good food from fresh ingredients."
—Julia Child

Junk food may seem convenient and taste good, but even a little of it goes a long way in upsetting my intentions to eat healthy food and take care of the body God has given me. I know that my good intentions need to include awareness of whether the food I eat is nutritious.

God has also given me wisdom, and I use it to determine if I am getting enough calories, vitamins, and minerals to be healthy. If I need to learn more about the basics of nutrition, there is plenty of information—at bookstores, libraries, and on the Internet. I might even learn to cook food that not only nourishes me but also tastes good.

Eating simply because I am tired, bored, or upset instead of when I'm hungry can become a habit. Instead, I listen within for guidance, and I make food choices that will energize and satisfy me for several hours, rather than for just a short time after a meal.

Nourishing my body with healthful foods in
the right portions, I am energized and also satisfied.

NEVER ALONE

—◆—

"Every day affirm: I am never alone. I can do my job well. With God's help I can succeed. I am a positive thinker and believer."
—John Glossinger

Working or playing in the extreme heat outdoors, I can become dehydrated. But oh, how great it feels when I drink from a tall glass of cool water. The effects are immediate and soothing, as if my body is telling me, "YES!"

I get that same feeling of relief when, in the middle of a challenge, I remember that God is with me.

Friends and family love me, but that's no guarantee that an occasional argument won't flare up between us, leaving me feeling miserable and lonely. But I'm never really alone. God is with me—at all times. If I feel like I'm being hassled by someone, I know that God is right here to pick me up and help me shrug off the hurt. If I'm going for a job interview and feeling nervous, I remember that God is with me, so I keep my head high and my confidence up. Wherever I go, or whatever the challenge I am facing, I am never alone.

With a welcome sense of relief,
I remember that God is with me.

SAYING GOODBYE

—◆—

"I thank my God every time I remember you,
constantly praying with joy in every one
of my prayers for all of you."
—Philippians 1:3

Aloha can mean either goodbye or hello, depending upon the occasion. The word *goodbye* is a shortened version of the blessing, "God be with you."

I may say goodbye to my family and friends by saying, "See you soon" or "See you later." With this way of saying goodbye, I am telling them I have faith that we will be back together again and that I am looking forward to just that. When I say "goodbye," I am affirming that even though we are going to be some distance from one another, God is with my loved ones and with me, too. No matter how far apart we may be, just the same way that we will always see the same sun and moon, we will always share the same love of God.

Even when someone I care about is moving far away, I know that we are as close to each other as a prayer. And because we are eternally linked by the spirit of God, no goodbye is a final ending.

No matter how far the distance is between us,
my friends and I are close in prayer.

COMMITMENTS

◆

*"Desire is the key to motivation, but it's determination
and commitment to an unrelenting pursuit of your goal—
a commitment to excellence—that will enable you to attain
the success you seek." —Mario Andretti*

It seems that the list of my commitments grows with each passing year. Some of my commitments are easier to keep than others, especially the ones that I enjoy doing and believe are important.

If I have a commitment to a job after school, I am on time and I do the best work I can, because others are depending on me.

In all of my relationships, I am committed to growing and developing a loving, lasting connection—whether it is with someone I am dating on a regular basis or with my mom and dad. Each relationship requires a dedication on my part to be kind and loving.

My number one commitment is to God, which means that I am choosing to live a spiritual life with time set aside for prayer and meditation. In prayer with God, I receive the strength and wisdom to keep all of my commitments.

*God gives me the strength I need
to keep my commitments.*

SAY YES!
—◆—

*"God does not ask your ability or your inability . . .
only your availability."*
—Mary Kay Ashe

When I invite God to show me how I can be a blessing
to others, God answers with wonderful opportunities
that appear in my life. Then it is up to me to say "yes" to
expressing my God-given gifts.

I know that the opportunities that come to me are
provided by God in answer to prayer, and God knows I
am capable of doing what is required. Something might
seem really hard or even impossible to me, but God
knows it *is* possible.

What a tremendous feeling of satisfaction I receive
from knowing that I am using the skills that God has
given me. I am willing to do what God knows I can do.
And God answers my willingness by offering me even
more opportunities to shine.

I am blessed with wonderful experiences when I
simply say "yes" to expressing the divine light within me.

*I say "yes" to every God-given opportunity
to express the divine light within me.*

WITH GOD'S HELP

"God doesn't require us to succeed;
He only requires that we try."
—Mother Teresa

There is a divine plan unfolding through me. I may not know what it is right now, but I do know that I can count on God to help me along the way to discovering it. Even though I know that God is helping me, I don't rely on my Creator to do the work for me. This saying sums it up for me: "God provides the milk, but not the pail."

Opportunities are out there, and it's up to me to keep exploring them. With God's help I will not only find them, but I will discover more about myself. With God's help I see the potential within me, and I see myself in a new light. Do I need courage to speak to someone I want to meet? Knowing I am God's child gives me the self-esteem I need. Am I confused about what I want to do with my life after I graduate? God is with me through the decision-making process.

What a great feeling it is to know that the power that created the world is helping me now.

God loves me and is ready to help me
every minute of the day and night.

MEDITATION
I Believe

◆

Finding time during the day to meditate is a choice that I make, and one I am committed to keeping, because I believe in it. I believe that now, as I close my eyes and connect with Spirit Divine, I am energized by spiritual power.

Here in the quiet of my soul, I enjoy the sense of peace I feel when I talk one-on-one with God. While the outer me may thrive on being part of a social scene—enjoying movies, parties, or music—the inner me is refreshed by stillness.

With my eyes still closed and my mind still focused on God, I listen and hear only God. Here I can share my innermost feelings and know that God isn't going to judge me or tune me out.

I reveal my very deepest thoughts to God through my prayers and meditations with absolute assurance, because I know that God hears and answers my prayers.

I believe that God hears and answers
my prayers.

MAKING IT HAPPEN

Goals are important.
My long-term goals include:

_____

_____

_____

_____

_____

_____

_____

_____

_____

_____

_____

_____

BEING TRUE TO MYSELF

BY KATY

I'm a seventeen-year-old pastor's kid (otherwise known as a p.k.) who is going all-out in a career as a Christian singer and songwriter. Some people automatically assume that all p.k.'s get our kicks out of being bad and trying to always push the envelope. I do push the envelope, but I try to do it in a good way that actually gets me somewhere in life.

Being an attention-getting middle child, I was always in a race with my oldest sister to be the best. She started singing in our church, so a week later I started singing in church, also. I was nine, and a voice came out of me that I never realized I had. It's a God-given gift, but I've put a lot of practice toward my singing to make it perfect.

I eventually moved from singing along with tracks to accompanying myself on a guitar. Because I was a teenager who had something to say, I began writing my own songs. Later I began going on the road singing at festivals and making records.

As a part of the music industry at such a young age, I have had my ups and downs, but I have learned a lot. And a lot of what I have learned will help me in life. Hanging out with lots of cool people, people who have been my mentors, has influenced me in positive ways.

Being on the road is not easy for me, because I don't have the security and accountability of my friends around me. Not being in church as much as I would like to be, I'm trying to hold my own in having a career and in having a personal relationship with God.

My parents love that I'm doing what I'm doing for the Lord, not just to please them or others. They're constantly giving support, which is fantastic and a little overwhelming at times, because they want me to do every single gig. But I know I have to rest. I have been home-schooled and tested out of high school. I want to go to college, but I can't see that happening right now. So I'm taking one day at a time.

What I keep telling myself is to not become jaded with all that is happening career-wise. I realize that regardless of a career, I'm nothing without God. So my life right now is both a constant struggle and a constant triumph.

A lot of people compare me to Jennifer Napp or mainstream artists such as Fiona Apple. I have these jazzy, smokey vocal cords! But I'm changing daily, because I'm still a teenager in the process of finding out who I am and what my music is. I'm growing constantly—going through a youth's edition of a workbook about experiencing God.

As with all teens, it's important for me to be true to myself and not change who I am for other people. The hardest thing for me is to keep my ear open for God's voice. So many times I let too many people's opinions in. When this happens, my mind becomes corrupted with their voices when the only one that truly matters is God's—and sometimes my parents', because they are the ones who are paying the rent! To keep my mind true and clear, I keep a prayerful heart, a heart soft enough so that God can mold it in the way He wants it to be.

FORGIVE

◆

*"Forgiveness is the scent that the rose leaves
on the heel that crushes it."*
—Unknown

I don't know who actually feels better when I forgive
someone and move on with our relationship—the other
person or me.

Forgiveness does stir up happier feelings inside me,
lifting some really heavy and sometimes silly thoughts
from my mind. Once I have decided that I want to forgive
a friend, my brother or sister, or my parents, I can hardly
wait to tell them. I might not say it in a formal way. I
might just say "I forgive you" with a hug or by making
such a funny face that they can't help but laugh.

What causes me to want to forgive? I think it must be
God, nudging me forward to share the love that is in my
heart rather than the anger that might be in my mind. I
appreciate that, because there are times I need to forgive
myself, and I figure that if I can forgive others, I can
forgive myself. That feels really good, too.

*I feel so good when I forgive,
because I am giving love from my heart.*

Daily Word for Teens

How Sweet It Is

*"I am beginning to learn that it is the sweet,
simple things of life which are the real ones after all."*
—Laura Ingalls Wilder

My first thoughts when I woke up this morning might have been of all the things I needed to do today. Whether it's a school day or a Saturday, there are always several things on my to-do list.

Tonight when I am falling asleep, I could review the day, measuring my day's worth by how much I got accomplished. Instead, I plan on measuring today by its sweetness. I will remember the smiles that were given to me and returned by me, the food that I enjoyed, each "I love you" that was shared between myself and a special person in my life, every gift of comfort and reassurance that I gave or received. As I lay my head on my pillow tonight, I will end my day by measuring the sweet thought of the whole night of rest and dreams that await me, and the brand-new day that lies ahead.

How good it is to fall asleep with this thought about life: How sweet it is!

*I measure the success of today by the sweetness
of God's blessings.*

HONORING ONE ANOTHER

---◆---

"What are human beings that you are mindful of them . . . ?
You have made them for a little while lower than the angels;
you have crowned them with glory and honor."
—Hebrews 2:6–7

It's nice to be honored, to be appreciated by others and have them mention some of the things I am good at doing. I think of how God has honored all people, including me, by creating each living, breathing, thinking being and then giving each one of us a sacred spirit that is capable of expressing divine qualities!

When I hear or see news reports of people harming one another, I wonder how in the world people can be so unaware of how special each and every person is. I wish I could make a satellite broadcast to the world, encouraging everyone to honor one another.

For now, I will do my part by honoring God and honoring all that God has created. All people are special to God and deserve to be appreciated and in some way told how special they are. I can do that, right where I am in the world!

I honor God by honoring every person
as a creation of the Creator.

HOW I FEEL

—◆—

"Feel the feeling. Choose the behavior."
—Charles Rumberg

Excitement and peace, sadness and joy, guilt and freedom—it's amazing how many different feelings I can have in just one day! I give myself permission to feel the way I feel, but I choose to act on my feelings in loving, responsible ways.

I check my own emotions by asking myself, "how and what am I feeling?" I name each feeling and bless it for calling my attention to something that I might need to change—or accept—in my life. Then I let the feeling float on through my mind without dwelling on it. Sometimes I just need to push past a feeling such as dread about starting my homework and just do it!

I realize that feelings are not always based on reality, so I check out the facts before I act on my feelings. If an adjustment needs to be made, I make it. Considering how my actions and words might affect others, I choose the most loving ways to express myself.

I am aware of my feelings, and I act on them
in loving, responsible ways.

WAKE UP!

—◆—

*"I would rather be a superb meteor, every atom of me
in magnificent glow, than a sleepy and permanent planet."*
—Jack London

There have been times when I could have put my head down and slept right through a class—and maybe I did! I could choose to sleep my way through life, too, but I know there is an extraordinary day waiting for me as I wake up and open my eyes to the wonder of life all around me.

Living with spiritual awareness, I am awake. My life makes a leap to a whole new level of meaning. I discover that God really is everywhere present—in the kind words of a friend, in a seeming coincidence that shows there is divine order in everything, in the deeper truths I now see revealed in a movie.

When I live each day from this higher level of awareness, I am seeing with spiritual eyes, noticing the sparkling details of life I hadn't been aware of before. I begin to realize that living a spiritual life is anything but boring or limiting. I am waking up to an extraordinary future as a spiritual being.

*I wake up and open my eyes to the wonder of life
that is all around me.*

COMMUNICATION

———◆———

"Communication is a two-way street. And while we revel in the reality that we can always get through to heaven, our concern should be whether our Lord can always get through to us."
—Joseph Stowell

Communication between people can glide along as smoothly as a luxury car and zip along as fast as a sports car. Yet like the smoothest or fastest car, communication can break down.

So it's important that my communication be in top form. I want to say what I really mean to say in the way I mean to say it, so I tune up my communication skills by listening carefully to what I say and how it sounds.

When I do listen, I may be surprised to hear that one of my simple statements takes on an unfriendly tone. I can and do correct that. And sometimes what I feel the most is hardest for me to say. I may feel embarrassed saying "I love you" to someone I really love, but when I do say it, I am so glad that I communicated what I am honestly feeling. I always will be true to myself when I respond from the love of God that is within me.

I express the love of God within my heart
when I communicate.

MEDITATION

Inner Peace

◆

Sometimes, when I am listening to my favorite music, I feel it as much as I hear it. I have tuned in with more than my ears. When I meditate, I tune out all the sounds and scenes outside me and tune in to what is inside me:

In the quiet, I move to a depth where something beyond my usual senses kicks in. When I think of a flower, I can smell its sweet fragrance. When I think of wading in a clear stream, I feel a sensation of cool water swirling around my feet.

Going even deeper in thought to God, I know the presence of God with every fiber of my being. Peace moves through me to soothe every hurt of the past and wash them away. I see myself radiating peace. I know that I can be at peace no matter what is going on around me.

I bring the peace of God back with me, knowing that I am embraced and sustained by it.

The peace of God blesses me
with a serenity of the soul.

GRATITUDE

The people and things I
am most thankful for are:

_____

_____

_____ Thank You,
_____ God, for:

_____

_____

_____

_____

_____

_____

_____

_____

_____

_____

PROSPERITY

——◆——

"I keep the telephone of my mind open to peace, harmony, health, love and abundance. Then, whenever doubt, anxiety, or fear try to call me, they will keep getting a busy signal."
—Edith Armstrong

A certain kind of jeans, that newly released CD, those cool shoes I keep thinking about—it seems like there is always something new that I just have to have! It's easy to get caught up in thinking about what I don't have— especially when my family may be going through financial challenges. But instead of wanting more, I think about *doing* more. I can contribute to my family's finances with a part-time job, and I can also contribute to our well-being with my attitude of prosperity thinking.

I take time to notice what I *do* have and to be thankful for it all. I practice sharing my good fortune with others and celebrating their successes. I speak positively about money, reminding myself and my family that God always provides exactly what we need. I'm learning that God's universe has more than enough for everyone, and I am ready to receive!

I am open and ready to receive the good that God has prepared for me.

On Time

*"The angels always deliver blessings.
And they are never, ever late."*
—LeRoy White

Reminders for me to be on time are everywhere, from the alarm clock that goes off early on a school day, to the bell that rings when class starts, to parents nudging me to finish my homework or go to bed. I seem to have to work pretty hard at being on time!

There is another kind of time, and that is God's time. I imagine the divine timing that it must take to answer every prayer and send out every blessing. Then I smile, knowing that God is always on time. I might wish that the good things I'm praying for will happen sooner, but then I relax and trust God. I understand that all will happen at just the right time.

God's plan is unfolding. My parents might remind me about my homework—but if they are ever worried about a challenging situation, *I* reassure *them:* God's plan is right on time!

*I am trusting and patient, because God's blessings
are always right on time.*

THANKFULNESS

—◆—

*"Sometimes we need to remind ourselves
that thankfulness is indeed a virtue."*
—William Bennett

Today, I think I'll start a trend by making my own corner of the world even better. Today I'll not only be thankful for the people in my life, but I will also express my thankfulness to them.

I can start out with my immediate family. In his or her own way, each member of my family helps me out—with laundry, a home-cooked meal, or a ride somewhere. Today I let them know with my words and actions that I am thankful to have them in my life.

As I go about my day, I act on any opportunity I have to say "thanks" to anyone. Whether it's a friend sharing a funny story with me or a clerk at the mall giving me my change, I smile and say "Thanks." The more I use it, the more my new thankful attitude becomes a part of my everyday life. With each "thanks," I am adding to a lifetime of good feelings.

*Today I let others know
how thankful I am.*

Daily Word for Teens

SPIRITUAL GROWTH
— ◆ —

"God enters by a private door into every individual."
—Ralph Waldo Emerson

Some people appear to have such strong faith and peace of mind that they never get flustered or upset. I can have that same kind of faith and presence of mind by relying fully on the wisdom of God to guide me. Each day I am a seeker who wants to discover more in my relationship with God. As I explore, my spiritual understanding grows. I am on a quest to learn more about what God can achieve through a willing soul.

I receive greater understanding through prayer. I also learn by hearing about the experiences of others, by attending a prayer group at my church, or by reading books on spirituality.

I want whatever I learn to help me have a closer walk with God, so I choose what speaks to my soul. My relationship with God is a sacred, personal one. As I open my mind and heart to the truth of my oneness with God, I cannot help but experience spiritual growth.

*I am on a quest to grow spiritually
by including more of God in my life.*

Daily Word for Teens

FLEXIBLE

"I can do all things through him who strengthens me."
—Philippians 4:13

I can honestly say that I'm impressed at how flexible I can be, because I seem to always be adjusting to something new and changing. Being flexible is proving to be one of my strengths.

Going from one classroom to another and shifting my thinking every hour from one subject to another can be especially hard at the beginning of a school year. As I go with the flow of learning a new routine, meeting new people, and learning new information, I can handle it all.

What probably helps me the most is that before I walk up to a new group or walk into a new classroom, I say a little prayer: "God, help me make new friends and help me learn what I need to know."

Knowing that God is with me as I open the door to the classroom and say "hi" to that group gives me confidence!

*I am flexible and strong, because I know
that this is how God created me to be.*

COMMUNITY

◆

"We are the environment."
—Charles Panati

The kids at school, my circle of friends, my family, and I create the environment within our community. We are all different colors and sizes. We have varied interests and hobbies. We keep our community open and flourishing with diversity when we accept that we are each unique and important.

I know that the people and conditions within my home and school, my neighborhood and world have influenced me in positive ways. And I also want to be a positive influence for others. Together we are building a greater understanding of one another.

Because I understand God's intention of good for all, I want to do all I can to bless the people who make up my community. What I can always do is let my words and actions help create an environment of love and acceptance that acknowledges and welcomes everyone as essential to the overall good of the community.

I am a positive influence on my community
and my community is a positive influence on me.

Daily Word for Teens

MEDITATION
Healthy and Whole

◆

Being healthy and whole is about more than the condition of my mind and body. It also concerns the condition of my soul. In fact, when I nourish my soul through prayer and meditation, I am practicing a great health routine:

First, I quiet my mind and think peaceful thoughts. As I do, I feel my body start to relax. With every thought, I send the message "relax" to the muscles of my neck and shoulders, my arms and legs.

I reach a state in which I am no longer aware of my body. I have moved within to the sanctuary of my soul. The more I think about God's spirit being there, the more quiet my thoughts become. Yes, I am in touch with God and my own spirituality. Totally immersed in the presence of God, I take a deep breath and release it. I am ready to take on the day as a healthy and whole person.

In touch with God and my own spirituality, I express
health and wholeness of spirit, mind, and body.

MY LIFE STORY...SO FAR

Writing the story of my life, I would include
the following chapters:

_____

_____

_____

_____

_____

_____

_____

_____

_____

_____

_____

_____

_____

BLESSINGS IN ALL THINGS

BY TREVOR

My mother and father divorced when I was two years old, but my life was fairly normal until the end of my freshman year in high school. By then a whole bunch of small things—personal and financial—had contributed to my mother, myself, and two younger sisters being homeless.

We had lost our home and most of our personal property. The two things that we still had that were of any value were a Suburban and an old computer. So for the next three years, we lived in our Suburban, with friends, or at a campsite.

For the first year, my sisters and I continued in public school. I did fairly well, but I was not an extraordinary student. Then at the end of my sophomore year, we decided that in order to be more flexible in our daily schedule and to not have to change schools so often, we would start home-schooling with our mom as our teacher. About that same time, we were staying with relatives, and through their church we were introduced to the Bible and the basics of Christianity.

Although we continued to be homeless, things seemed to get easier for us. We had gotten so accustomed to being homeless that having material things didn't matter. Growing in our Christianity did matter, because it gave us greater strength.

I did well in home-schooling. At the end of my junior year, I had taken three different standardized tests and made a perfect score on each one. Those perfect scores got me a lot of attention—from the media and people in general. The reason I took these tests was to show that I was actually learning in home-schooling. I wasn't surprised by the perfect scores I had made, and I don't really consider them a great achievement of mine so much as a result of my simply using an ability that God had given me.

Because of my test scores, I have gotten scholarship offers. I'd like to go to college and major in physics, because it's something I'm really interested in and feel I'm good at. I am letting the Lord lead me to the college that is right for me.

My family is no longer homeless. We are renting a one-bedroom apartment, and we really like it, because it serves all our needs.

I really respect my mother for the way she's concentrated on helping my sisters and me. One thing that she has often said is that she would much rather we have good character than do well academically. She's done a good job teaching us academically and of teaching us character.

Growth in character was necessary for us to make it through the trials of being homeless. We know that if anything bad happens to us again, we have the ability to get through it as long as we have faith in God.

One of my favorite Bible verses is Romans 8:28: "We know that all things work together for good for those who love God, who are called according to his purpose." Basically that scripture is the story of my life. I would like for everyone to know that whenever bad things happen, by continuing to have faith in God, those seemingly bad things can be turned into blessings.

CENTERED

—◆—

"My roots go down, down to the ground."
—Sarah Pirtle

The deep roots of a large oak tree hold it securely in place even in the strong winds of a thunderstorm. I imagine the tree receiving its strength from the nurturing, nutrient-rich soil below its branches. The roots reach deeper within the earth with each growing season. Without this root system the tree would not receive the nutrients it needs to grow, and it would surely topple over.

Just like the oak tree, I, too, am able to stay balanced and centered. When I pray, my awareness turns deep within my soul to find the foundation of God's love that supports me. Being with God in quiet, calm prayer nurtures my soul and keeps me strong in the face of challenges.

As I pray through the difficult times in my life, I am growing in inner strength and flexibility. With my awareness firmly rooted in God's presence deep within, I can withstand any stormy situation.

I am strong and flexible, because my awareness is firmly centered in God's presence.

MY BOUNDARIES

— ◆ —

"Trust your hunches. They're usually based on facts filed away just below the conscious level."
—Dr. Joyce Brothers

Even if I don't own many material things, I do own three things that are priceless: my own body, my own thoughts, and my own feelings.

My actions are sometimes limited by rules and policies—and sometimes my parents are the rule-makers. But I decide what I think and feel.

I also decide who I choose to have physically near me, and how close I allow them to be. I trust divine intuition within me as I decide who to let in to my personal space. I make wise choices based on self-respect, self-discipline, and good judgment.

If I feel uncomfortable because of others' behavior, I tell them so. If they persist, I honor myself by asking for help from a trusted adult.

My body, my thoughts, and my feelings are treasures from God. I own the right to decide whether and how I share them with others. With God's strength and guidance, I define my own boundaries.

My body, my thoughts, and my feelings
are priceless gifts from God.

Daily Word for Teens

My Thoughts
Are Prayers

—◆—

*"Every good thought you think is contributing its share
to the ultimate result of your life."*
—Grenville Kleiser

When I pray, I am talking to God. And God is always listening to me with love, whether I am praying or not. Every time I think a positive thought, I am expressing a kind of prayer.

My thoughts today help to shape my future days. If I am thinking pleasant thoughts about a friend and seeing the good in him or her, my future experiences with that friend are more likely to be pleasant. I know that it's up to me to choose to see the good in a person or a situation.

My thoughts are like previews of what I would like to see happen. I ask myself: do I really like what I see? Am I imagining the best, or am I worrying about the worst that could happen? I am not the Maker of the world I live in, but I do decide how I choose to *see* that world.

Every positive thought I have is a prayer, and I am mindful to hold positive, peaceful thoughts.

*My thoughts are powerful, positive expectations
of good things to come.*

KIND

*"No act of kindness, no matter how small,
is ever wasted."*
—Aesop

Thinking back on yesterday or the day before, I review how kind and considerate I was—or wasn't. Today I choose to express kindness and compassion to everyone—especially new kids in my neighborhood and school, because they might be feeling uneasy about their new surroundings.

The kindness and love of my family and friends can carry me through the most difficult times. A kind word or act clears away frustration and anger and replaces them with acceptance and joy.

Kindness seems to have a life of its own. When I make the choice to be kind to others, they may be encouraged to be kind to the people they meet. Then those people act kindly toward still others. And so it goes until my original act of kindness has multiplied many times over and blessed countless others. Acts of kindness are ongoing, and there is no limit to their ability to bless.

*My acts of kindness are multiplied
in a growing circle of goodwill.*

NEW DOORS

*"If you view all the things that happen to you,
both good and bad, as opportunities, then you operate
out of a higher level of consciousness."*
—Les Brown

In a blink of an eye, changes in my life may present choices as new doors of opportunity open before me. But which one should I go through?

The last thing I want to do is let myself get caught up in a rush to do something. So before I take any steps, I first consult with my higher power—God. God and God alone can guide me to the way that I should go.

Today is a new day in which I can turn from having no direction to having and holding on to a new opportunity that may ultimately change the direction of my entire life. As I continue through new doors, I will always be in the company of and under the guidance of God.

God encourages me to stretch my limits—to reach to new heights and to grasp the world as if with both hands, joyfully proclaiming, "Yes, I can!"

I live my life in gratitude for each new door of opportunity that God opens before me.

*God encourages me to believe in myself
and to go through new doors of opportunity.*

ALWAYS LOVED

"To love and be loved is to feel the sun from both sides."
—David Viscott

Something so subtle as a person's lack of interest in me and what I feel passionate about can cause me to feel unappreciated or misunderstood. When I think it over, I know that underneath it all I am probably feeling unloved. And it's natural to want to be loved!

In a quiet meditation time with God, I dedicate myself to knowing more about true love. Then I am able to feel the love that is within me. I realize that real love is not something that comes and goes. Love is a constant element in the universe, like the air I breathe. Love is everywhere!

The bottom line is this: All love comes *from* God, even though it often comes *through* other people in my life. And God always loves me! Because I know this truth, I don't let myself become down about the bumps along the road of life.

God loves me always, and what greater love could there be?

The love of God strengthens and upholds me.
I am loved and I act in loving ways toward others.

Daily Word for Teens

My Spiritual Identity

◆

Here is a meditation I can use to get in touch with my true spiritual nature. I close my eyes, releasing the tension in my body. I let go of all the stresses and worries of the day. Next, I pretend that my appearance, my activities—even my name—belong to a character in a play. I am playing a role in the theater of life.

I imagine setting aside everything I know about this character: all of the things he or she does at school, his or her skills and abilities, talents, and favorite things. All of these are good, but I set them aside just for now. I allow myself to feel free of any definition of myself except that I am a creation of God. I imagine that I am a radiant being. I notice that I positively glow with love and light. This is the real me, the eternal me.

I come back to resume the play through my daily activities, sure of my true spiritual identity.

My true spiritual identity is unchanging and eternal: I am made of God's light and love.

MY PLACE

I have a favorite imaginary place where I go to meditate
and to be with God. This is how I describe it:

_____

_____

_____

_____

_____

_____

_____

_____

_____

_____

_____

_____

DIRECT LINE TO GOD

◆

"He is not far from each one of us. 'For in him
we live and move and have our being.'"
—Acts 17:27–28

Calling card, speed dial, cell phone, pager, Internet connection—there are so many ways I can stay connected with the people I love. Just a touch of a button puts me in contact. I can find out what I need to know, or I can hear someone say "I love you" or "It's going to be all right."

Even better, I have a direct line to God just by being still and calling on the presence of God right inside me. I don't have to memorize a phone number. I never get a busy signal or an answering machine. I don't have to charge a battery, and I don't need coins. Instantly, wherever I am, I am connected to God.

I can call God in prayer to ask questions and get the answers I need. I can take a few minutes to connect with God when I am feeling lonely or scared. I can call on God when I feel lost and need to know where to turn. Best of all, I can use that direct line when I just want to be reminded that God loves me.

My connection with God is just a prayer away,
because God is always here with me.

Good Company

"A true friend is one soul in two bodies."
—*Aristotle*

Odds are, my parents haven't always given their stamp of approval to all of my friends in the past. But my parents have taught me to use wisdom and good judgment about who I decide to hang out with. When I'm with my close-knit group of friends, I know I'm in good company, because they are people I respect and trust.

I'm sure that my friends feel the same about me. They choose to be with me because they enjoy being with me, and they trust and respect me. I act and speak with the kindness and consideration that I expect my friends to show toward me. It feels great to know that I am a true friend, too!

Whoever my friends are, they have God's spirit within them. I remember this when I bring my friends to meet my mom and dad. I am confident that my parents will accept them, because I have chosen the good company of true friends.

*When my friends and I are together,
we are in good company!*

Daily Word for Teens

JOY!

◆

"Joy is the feeling of grinning on the inside."
—Dr. Melba Colgrove

If I were playing a word association game and heard the word "happiness," what would first pop into my mind? Would I think of my family, my friends, a pet, or maybe that one special person in my life?

From one day to the next, the people and things that bring me happiness vary, depending on circumstances or my mood. This may be true, but there is a constant in my life that brings me the greatest joy of all—my relationship with God.

Being God-centered, I have my own source of joy within, and I express it through smiles and laughter, as spontaneity and enthusiasm. When I share joy, I inspire myself and others.

I look at life with a positive perspective, and I think thoughts of joy and happiness. Because I know that my thoughts affect my actions, I act in loving, constructive ways so that I do make a positive difference in my world.

*My thoughts are filled with joy,
and I radiate happiness.*

Daily Word for Teens

MOTIVATION

—◆—

*"To love what you do and feel that it matters—
how could anything be more fun?"*
—Katharine Graham

I am told so much of what I must do or should do that
there are times I want to shout, "For a change, just let
me do something *I* want to do!" Of course, I have no
trouble being motivated when I love what I am doing, as
long as I don't become distracted by something I love to
do even more.

And there are other times I need to be motivated to do
the simplest of things. Do I really want to get up when
the alarm goes off and go to school? Well, there are
friends I want to talk with and that novel we will be
discussing in class is proving to be entertaining. . . . So
being a self-motivator, I talk myself into getting up.

I am moving ahead, making progress in life, and I
realize the importance of being motivated. I am thankful
when it comes naturally, and I am also willing to let my
greatest motivation be in realizing that the spirit of God
enlivens me. God always responds when I call for greater
motivation.

*My motivation comes from loving what I do
and from asking God to inspire me to do even more.*

SPIRITUAL PRINCIPLES

*"Open my eyes, so that I may behold
wondrous things out of your law."
—Psalms 119:18*

Swimming upstream in a strong current doesn't get me very far, and takes a lot of effort! But flowing with the stream is easy. So I work with, not against, the physical laws that govern my environment.

Just like there are principles of physics that govern my outer environment, there are spiritual principles that influence my inner world. They create a strong current of positive energy that I can use to make things easier for myself. One spiritual principle is that the universe has enough good things for me and for everyone to have what we need. When I live from this truth and work with it, I begin to easily attract God's good. Another spiritual principle is that God loves me unconditionally. When I am aware of this truth and flow with it, I naturally share my awareness with others through my loving words and actions.

I work with the positive energy of God's spiritual principles, and I bring about positive results.

*I work with God's spiritual principles to create blessings
in my life and in the lives of others.*

MAKING A DIFFERENCE

"There are admirable potentialities in every human being.
Believe in your strength and your youth.
Learn to repeat endlessly to yourself, 'It all depends on me.'"
—Andre Gide

I can and do make a difference in my world, right where I am, every day. Such a simple thing as being courteous to my parents, teachers, and the people I meet on my after-school job is a statement that tells the truth about teens: we *are* thoughtful and caring.

What other kinds of differences do I want to make? Does caring for the very young or the elderly hold a special place in my heart? Is the welfare of pets and other animals something that I act on now and plan as a career in the future? Do I have a desire to express my acceptance of all people for who they are as God's precious creations, deserving of every consideration and the highest respect?

There is no limit to the difference of good that I can make in my world. The more I think about it, the more I think to include. And I thank God that with my Creator's help I can make a difference—today and every day!

I make a difference in my world by being
a loving, caring child of God.

Daily Word for Teens

MEDITATION
Decisions

◆

Making a decision on the spur of the moment is not a comfortable or even a reliable thing to do. Yet when someone is pressuring me to say or do something or when an immediate decision is indicated, I need to escape for a moment, and I do:

In a sacred retreat, I shut out all noises from outside of me, and I go in thought and prayer to that peaceful center within me. This is where I give the situation to God, and I silently affirm: *In the presence of God there is no rush to make a decision; there is only peace and love.*

I draw on the wisdom of the universe in my sacred retreat, and a silent message of assurance tells me that God guides me and supports me in making all decisions. My decision to first call on God for guidance and support enables me to make the very best decisions and to feel confident about making them.

In a sacred retreat with God, I receive the wisdom needed to make the very best decisions.

WHERE DO I FIT IN?

Like everyone else, I want to find my place
in the world. I see my place and purpose as:

_____

_____

_____

_____

_____

_____

_____

_____

_____

_____

_____

A Second Chance

By Danielle

Although I didn't know at age fourteen what it was called, I was struggling with a form of depression called dysthymia. The next two years were extremely hard for me, because I didn't know who to talk to or even what to say in order to get help. I didn't think that anybody could possibly understand what I was going through, so I more or less isolated myself from others.

My parents were so worried about me that they sent me to a counselor. I felt frustrated with the counseling sessions, because I wasn't feeling any better. One day I was in my bedroom, doing my homework. Feeling angry, frustrated, guilty, and sad, I was in a lot of pain emotionally. As I used a compass to complete a math problem, a thought popped into my head: "Hurt yourself." I tried to ignore it, but the thought wouldn't go away. So I did something that was my first step on a journey of self-mutilation: I made 10 to 14 deep scratches in my arms with the sharp point of my compass. I spent that weekend wearing long sleeves and hiding in my room. I did e-mail one of my teachers, and she helped me make it through the weekend.

That following Monday, I told my counselor what had happened and ended up being under the strict supervision of my parents, seeing a shrink, going on medication, and having counseling every day.

I had become very antagonistic toward God and very angry on the inside. My freshman year, my mom and dad sent me to a church camp that my mom had attended as a teen, and I had an okay time. By the next summer, I was struggling even more, so Mom and Dad decided to send me back to camp.

This time I had a really awesome experience. I understood that the people there were all willing to listen to me, and I opened up and talked to them. They accepted me without ever condemning me for cutting myself. (I had an incident while at camp.) They showed me what true Christians are like, and I wanted to be like these people and to experience what they were experiencing, because they were so loving and happy.

The anger I had felt toward God before I came to camp that year was gone. I listened to my new friends talk about a God of love, a God who loved me. I accepted that God really did love me, and I found worth in that love.

I actually felt happy for the first time in years and realized I had a choice to make about my life: I could choose to be happy or to be sad. I chose happy. I had a long journey ahead of me after that summer at camp, and had several slips. But I kept going and declaring, "God is my strength!" My faith in God gave me the extra strength I needed to get through it.

I still have difficult times, especially in the summer when I'm out of school and my life is not so structured. I think each of us needs to know that even though we may struggle in our faith, we need to keep trying and not let doubt and worry get to us. In the end it doesn't matter whether we are popular or whether we are beautiful. It matters how much we know God and how much we love God. That kind of relationship with God makes life something worthwhile, something we cherish.

My depression has almost disappeared, thanks to medication, counseling, and a lot of work on my part. I haven't cut myself for several years. I have a deep sense of joy and peace that no one can take away from me. I have made friends and become active in my church.

From the first time I was asked the question, "What do you want be when you grow up?" my answer has always been, "An artist." I still want to be an artist, but now I have decided that I also want to be a counselor. I want to help teens know that depression isn't a shameful thing and that they don't have to go through anything alone. I have survived some things that nobody should ever have to go through, but God has given me a second chance at life. I am going to use that second chance to help others and to make the world a better place for us all.

God

By Laura

Everything is God
From the clouds in the sky
to the tears that we cry,
In the sway of the trees,
God's the little things that make us
weak in our knees.

God is in the words that we speak,
God sits upon every mountain's peak,
Watching us as we sleep and pray,
By our sides each night and each day.

Being one with God gives us a choice,
We can ignore His existence,
or we can hear His voice.

DIVINE ORDER

—◆—

"A well-ordered life is like climbing a tower;
the view halfway up is better than the view from the base,
and it steadily becomes finer as the horizon expands."
—William Lyon Phelps

When I hear the words "divine order," I sometimes wonder what they mean, and what they mean to me personally.

Looking in Webster's dictionary, I find that "divine" means "of, relating to, or proceeding directly from God," while "order" can mean "to put persons or things into their proper places in relation to each other." So I know that divine order is God guiding me to where I need to be when I need to be there.

I might not always feel the effects of divine order in my life, yet in the recesses of my soul I know it is real. It might not be quite as evident as the sun rising or the plants that produce oxygen for me to breathe, but it is there.

Divine order isn't an instant guarantee that things are going to work out how I want them to, but it does assure me that God's spirit is acting in and through me and everyone else, for the highest good of all.

Divine order is at work in my life.

STUDY BREAK

◆

"Don't panic!"
—*Douglas Adams,* The Hitchhiker's Guide to the Galaxy

Two history chapters to read, twenty math problems to solve, a test in science to study for, and an English paper to write—I've been there! With this much to catch up on, I might panic or be tempted to catch up on my TV-watching instead. But neither panicking nor putting off doing my homework will make me feel better.

Fortunately, I have a constructive way to take a break. I set the books and the worries aside. I close my eyes and breathe deeply, letting my body relax with each breath. I remember that I am more than a student of math, science, or history. I am a student of life, learning to stay centered in God's peace all the time. I ask God for help, and I reclaim all the energy I was using up worrying so that I can use it to make progress. I return from my study break to find that I can accomplish my work more easily when I am feeling peaceful and calm.

I am a student of life, learning to accomplish my goals calmly and peacefully.

KEEPING CONFIDENCES

---◆---

"If you reveal your secrets to the wind, you should not blame the wind for revealing them to the trees."
—Kahlil Gibran

I may get the attention of a group of friends if I repeat a secret told to me by someone outside the group. But I know that everyone who listened as I blabbed a secret would walk away from me knowing that I could never be trusted. And I would walk away sorry that I betrayed someone.

No, I won't let that happen! I care more about being a trustworthy person and friend than I do about getting the attention of others. Keeping a confidence is a sacred trust that I honor.

What happens when friends tell me something they are doing or planning to do that could cause them or others harm? I pray! I ask God to guide me to be the best possible friend I can be. If God gives me the go-ahead to talk to parents or teachers, I do, because I could save someone from harm. I honor my friends with my good judgment about keeping confidences.

With God guiding my judgment,
I honor the confidences of my friends.

FIRED UP!

*"Who would ever think that so much went on
in the soul of a young girl?"*
—Anne Frank

There is no mistaking it: I am fired up and ready for life. Others might not be aware that I am, but I *know* it! I have an inner enthusiasm about trying new adventures and even about doing the routine things in life, because I know that I live as a divine creation.

I might be thinking about redecorating my room so that it makes a definite statement about who I am. I might try out for a sports or debate team. Others might laugh if I were to tell them that I am my own cheerleader, but it's true. Being fired up means that I cheer myself on when I need some encouragement.

I have a lot of energy inside me to do and be everything that God has made me capable of doing and being. I affirm that I have a strong spirit, a sound mind, and a healthy body, and that I am eager to express the greatness that God has created me to express. When I realize that God is my Creator and that I am a divine being, I get fired up about life!

*I am ready and able to express the greatness
that God has created me to express.*

Daily Word for Teens

ATTRACTION

---◆---

*"You've got to get up every morning with a smile on your face
and show the world all the love in your heart. . . .
You're going to find . . . that you're beautiful as you feel."*
—Carole King

Standing in front of a mirror, I may wonder how others see me. Am I attractive? Do people like me when they meet me for the first time? Does that special someone I'm attracted to feel the same way about me?

Rather than letting self-doubt take over, I think about what attracts *me:* I am drawn to people who have qualities that I might like to have myself. So I pay attention to what attracts me, and I encourage myself to develop those same qualities.

I also see that many of the people I'm attracted to aren't necessarily as perfect-looking as a magazine cover model, but they are attractive to me when they seem happy with themselves the way they are.

I will probably never understand all of the mysteries of love and attraction, but I do know that I, too, am attractive—when I love and appreciate myself for who I am.

*I am attractive to others because I love
and appreciate myself.*

Daily Word for Teens

ONENESS

— ◆ —

"We, who are many, are one body in Christ,
and individually we are members one of another."
—Romans 12:4–5

Walking in nature, it's amazing how connected I feel to
life: the trees, the buzzing insects, the birds chirping
overhead. It's no wonder, because I really am one with
everything—and one with God.

When I think of God, I don't think of a being in human
form high up in the sky. God is so much greater and
closer to me than that!

In fact, I am surrounded by God's energy. God is inside
me and outside me. I am made up of the same energy as
God. Just like a drop of water is made up of the same
elements as the entire ocean, I am made up of the essence
of God. I am not God, just like the drop of water is not
the whole ocean. But like that little drop of water that
knows it is a part of the mighty ocean's power, I am at
home in God's loving presence.

Every form of life is a drop in that same ocean that is
God. We are one.

I am one with God and with all life.

MEDITATION
Freedom

◆

For my time of meditation today, I focus on the freedom I experience by living a life centered in God's presence.

As I go within in prayer, I acknowledge that even though God is actively at work in my life, I am still free to choose whether or not I act on that divine guidance. God does not force me to do anything or to act in any certain way. I give thanks for that freedom.

While keeping my breathing slow and steady, I continue to pray, and I feel a rush of inner peace. I have made a choice to live my life as a prayer, and I vow today to follow through on that choice.

"God, You have blessed me with a free spirit, and I accept this divine gift with gratitude and tremendous respect for the responsibility involved. You leave me free to choose, and I joyfully and enthusiastically choose You, O God."

Thank You, God,
for my gift of freedom.

MY PRAYER LIST

_____

_____

_____

_____

_____

_____

_____

_____

_____

_____

_____

_____

_____

Daily Word for Teens

PRAY FOR OTHERS

"I pray that, according to the riches of his glory . . . you may be strengthened in your inner being with power through his Spirit, and that Christ may dwell in your hearts through faith, as you are being rooted and grounded in love."—Ephesians 3:16, 17

I pray for my best friends, even though there are times when we don't see eye to eye. The beauty of true friendship is that it encourages us to quickly forgive one another and go on with our lives.

But how can I pray for someone with whom I have had a serious disagreement or for someone whose way of life and beliefs differ from my own? I can, because I know that we are all children of God, and the only thing that divides us as the family of God is the mistaken belief that we are separate from one another.

I pray that all anger being expressed in the world is replaced by the love of God, so that every home, neighborhood, and country is a safe haven—a place of acceptance and serenity for all.

As I pray for others, I am blessing the precious children of God—whether they are friends, family, or strangers—with thoughts of love, understanding, and compassion.

I pray for others knowing that we are all members of the family of God.

Daily Word for Teens

School Blessing

"No one can look back on his school days and say with truth that they were altogether unhappy."
—George Orwell

My school is much more than a place for learning. It's a place where I meet friends that I might keep for a lifetime, a place where I make plans for my future, and the place where I spend much of my time—my home away from home.

For these reasons, I ask God in my prayers to bless my school:

"God, bless this school and all who come here. As each student and teacher enters through these doors, I pray that we do so in a spirit of fellowship and understanding. May the teachers here be patient and kind, and my fellow students and I considerate and eager to learn.

"I know that Your love and guidance make this school a safe, secure place where I can study and enjoy times with friends. Thank You, God, for Your presence here, and thank You that my memories of this school will be happy ones."

As I go to school, I affirm that God is there, blessing all who enter.

LEADING BY EXAMPLE

—◆—

*"There are some people who have the quality of richness and joy
in them and they communicate it to everything they touch.
It is first of all a physical quality; then it is a quality of the spirit."*
—Thomas Wolfe

Even though I may not be a leader of a club or team,
others may look up to me because I live a life of integrity,
doing what I know is right and true for me. Or they
may admire and appreciate my friendly and loving nature.

I lead by example when I am successful, but also
when I allow others to see that I am learning and growing
from the mistakes I have made. Day by day, step by
step, I am improving myself and encouraging others to
do the same.

After all, being a leader doesn't mean that I am smarter
or better than anyone else. But because I have faith in
God and confidence in myself, I naturally make a positive
impression on others, and they learn from my example.

As my faith and confidence continue to grow, my life
is enriched, and by example I help to enrich the lives of
others.

*Each day I continue to grow in faith and in confidence
so that I do lead by example.*

TRUE PERFECTION

—◆—

*"Start thinking of yourself as an artist and your life
as a work-in-progress. Works-in-progress are never perfect.
But changes can be made. Art evolves."*
—Sarah Ban Breathnach

All through my life there have been times when I have
strived for perfection: coloring a whole page without
once going outside of the lines, getting 100% on a test,
scoring a 10 on the gymnastics team, weighing in at just
the "right" weight. And maybe I felt a little down when I
didn't succeed.

But God knows the truth about me: I *am* an example of
true perfection! That might sound hard to believe at first,
but then I realize that I don't have to be different from
who and what I am to be truly perfect. I am perfect just
the way I am: a learning, growing child of God.
Sometimes I make mistakes, sometimes I get it exactly
right, but most of the time I get it somewhere in between.
My body, my knowledge, my skills, my spirituality—
every part of me is constantly evolving. I am truly perfect
in God's eyes, because I am the ongoing creation that
God designed me to be.

*I am perfect the way I am: an ongoing, learning,
evolving creation of God.*

Daily Word for Teens

FOREVER YOUNG

—◆—

"I am not young enough to know everything."
—Oscar Wilde

At times I think I can hardly wait to grow up. I am eager to take on new responsibilities and challenges. Then at other times I wonder just how in the world I will be able to work full time, pay my own bills, take care of my own place, and do so much more.

Being a teen, I have to admit I am young, but I know that my youthfulness inspires me to take chances and try different things. I seem to bounce back quickly from a challenge that an adult may consider a big deal. Yet I know some adults who are as adventurous as any teen, and who are great role models for staying youthful. They are willing to try and not make it and then go on to try again.

A youthful spirit is something that can last for a lifetime. I won't give it up as I grow older, because it serves me well. I know that I have an eternal youthfulness that springs from the spirit of God within me, no matter what my age may be.

My youthful spirit shows an eternal enthusiasm for life.

MY OWN STYLE

"A wonderful realization will be the day you realize that you are unique in all the world. . . . The world is an incredible unfulfilled tapestry. And only you can fulfill that tiny space that is yours."
—Leo Buscaglia

Thank God I am unique! I have my own style in the way that I dress and the way that I speak and interact with others. Even the way I decorate my bedroom is truly my own style.

I am like a window that allows the light of God within me to shine through. My style is like a colorful drapery that frames the light. And even though my outer style may change, the real me—that bright, warm, shining light within—never changes. The light within me sparks an attitude of confidence, encouraging me to express my own style and to act in ways that accentuate the inner spirit of God that is the real me.

Only I can be me, and I have a choice as to how I express the light of God within me through my own style. I celebrate my own uniqueness, and I appreciate all of the other unique expressions of God that I see in every other person.

I have my own unique style that celebrates the light of God within me.

MEDITATION
Comfort

◆

At the core of my being is a sacred place that no outer conflict or situation can invade—a place unblemished and pure with the holy spirit of God. Closing my eyes, I tune out the world and tune in to God. In my mind I envision a beautiful gate leading into a fragrant, colorful garden filled with every type of flower imaginable. Opening the gate, I enter this holiest of places, knowing that God waits for me there.

I feel God's loving presence enfolding me like a cloak. Gone are the feelings of doubt that I came in here with and forgotten are the past hurts that I have carried with me all along. God takes them from me and lovingly assures me that I need not worry about them any more.

In this garden of prayer, I am in a place of comfort where no one or no thing can disturb my peace. Even after I leave this place and continue about my day, I am at peace knowing that I can come back at any time.

Turning to God in prayer,
I enter a sacred garden of peace.

Daily Word for Teens

THIS IS THE YEAR

By my next birthday, I want to have achieved
some of the following:

_____

_____

_____

_____

_____

_____

_____

_____

_____

_____

_____

_____

_____

_____

Friends, Family, and Faith

By Rob

I had never been in such a deep meditation before. It was during a church youth group conference in August 1998. We were listening to a musician playing a twenty-minute percussion solo using many different kinds of drums. I closed my eyes, and even though I stayed awake, I felt as if I was falling asleep. When I meditate, I'm so alert, yet never more relaxed. This time it was as if I was disconnecting from the auditorium filled with people. I began to see a vision, like little flickers in my mind. In my vision I saw myself surrounded by the 500 teenagers and adults at the conference. Then several people from the crowd lifted me up and set me down on my feet. I began to walk. This may not seem remarkable, but it was to me, because I was born with a birth defect called spina bifida. I am paralyzed from the waist down.

When I came out of the meditation, I was shaking. The idea of walking, even with crutches, would be a giant leap of faith. Yet I knew that somehow I wanted to make this vision a reality. I immediately told several friends about it. Not once did any of them discourage me. All I got was, "Yes, do it! Go!"

I came home from the conference in a euphoric state and

told my parents, "Guess what? I'm going to walk!" They were a little anxious about what I wanted to do. I'm a singer, and they've always supported me in my music career and whatever else I wanted to do, but this time they brought me back to reality a bit.

After much debate, my mom and I went to the orthopedic surgeon I'd seen when I was five. I had to wear a hospital gown and sit in a cramped room on an exam table covered with that deli-paper they use. The doctor finally came in and I said, "I want the chance to walk." When he gave me some unreasonable alternatives, I asked for a referral to another doctor.

I wasn't disappointed—I was angry. But still, that appointment was just one obstacle.

In October the minister at my church heard about what I wanted to do, and she called me up to the platform in front of the whole congregation to share my vision. I got everyone's prayer support. I felt their energy carrying me.

My mom, dad, and I went to the rehab specialist the surgeon had recommended. This time everything went perfectly. The room was large and bright—and no deli-paper! After five minutes, in walked a rehabilitation specialist, a physical therapist, a clinical psychologist, and a guy who makes braces.

I said, "I want to know how I can best use the muscles that I've got to walk." I braced myself for the 'no.' The doctor said, "Yeah. I see that as a possibility." I almost fainted. They said they thought I could take my first steps by New Year's Day. So I set that goal for myself. And on December 28, 1998, in my physical therapist's office, I

Daily Word for Teens

walked for the first time, and with every step I was thinking, "Thank You, God!"

In April 1999 my minister invited me back. She said to the congregation, "Back in October, we had Rob on stage asking for your help on his journey to walk. I'd like you to turn around to the back of the sanctuary and greet Rob." And I walked down the center aisle with my braces. Everybody was cheering! All my friends were there, going crazy. My mom was in tears, as usual, and trying to hold the video camera. My dad was sitting there saying, "I always knew this would happen." My sister's going, "That's my brother!" My doctor was there, too. It was a big shining moment. When I reached the stage, I thanked everybody that helped me.

At the youth conference in August, I surprised everyone by walking across the stage at the talent show. Once again, everybody was up on their feet, cheering and clapping. I walked off that stage and I got this feeling of, "Wow. I did it. I really did it." Afterward I had people coming up to me asking me about their challenges in life. Asking me! And that was overwhelming at first.

What really impacted me is the fact that I pushed the envelope. There is a certain limit where your body thinks that you can't do any more. And I pushed that limit. That's what I did. With the help of friends, family, and faith, that's exactly what I did.

Thank You, God

By Sarah

Dear God,

Thank You.

Thank You for the people and experiences that
    guide us and bless us throughout our lives.

Thank You for inspiration that fuels our souls.

Thank You for challenges that call us
    to rise higher.

Thank You for unlimited potential.

Thank You for Your faith in us, both when we
    believe in ourselves and when we don't.

Thank You for creating us in Your likeness.

Thank You for Your continuous connection to us.

Thank You for letting us do Your work here
    on Earth.

Thank You for the opportunity to love ourselves
    and others.

Thank You for the ability to forgive ourselves
    and others.

Thank You for letting all of these blessings be as
    much ours as Yours, for we are one.

Thank You for everything we are.

Thank You for everything.

Thank You, God.

Amen.

THANK YOU!

—◆—

*"In everyone's life, at some time, our inner fire goes out.
It is then burst into flame by an encounter with another
human being. We should all be thankful for those people
who rekindle the inner spirit."—Albert Schweitzer*

A thank-you can be my courteous response of appreciation to others for something thoughtful they said or did—such as someone telling me I look especially good that day or opening the door for me when my arms are full. Or a teacher, parent, or friend might have commented on the quality of a poem or paper I have written or a project I have put a lot of thought and effort into completing.

A heartfelt thank-you springs from me whenever I realize that someone has touched my day—my very life—in a wonderful and positive way.

Saying "thank you" allows me to express my gratitude and to acknowledge a person for an act of kindness and consideration. I never want to leave a thank-you unsaid, so I remember to thank those who have been kind to me. And I thank God for bringing people into my life who are expressions of God's love and care.

*I offer a thank-you to those who bless me, and to God
for bringing wonderful people into my life.*

LEAP OF FAITH

—◆—

"Some people see things as they are and ask 'why?'
I dream things that never were and ask 'why not?'"
—Robert F. Kennedy

Some days it seems that I am taking a leap of faith by just getting out of bed in the morning and going to school! If I'm facing a big test or an awkward situation at school, I might be tempted to pull the covers over my head and stay put. But I don't—I get out of bed with faith that because God is with me, I will do okay.

Watching others, I am amazed that some people seem to have it so together, while I am confused as to what to do or expect next. I get my own act together by focusing on the goals that I want to reach and by working toward meeting them. Even if it may seem to others that my goals are too high and unattainable, I take a leap of faith in myself and in God. Together God and I can do it!

There is a saying that might sound dated but is still true: Today is the first day of the rest of my life. So I meet it with faith!

I have faith in God and in what God and I
can do together.

POISE

—◆—

"Responsibility and resilience go together.
Winning and whining don't."
—Roger Crawford

When I'm riding a bike or jogging, I might find that going uphill can be challenging. Although I may be challenged physically and emotionally, I remain poised so that feelings of distress don't get in the way of my making it to the top. I know that for every uphill effort I have to make, there is a downhill side where the going will be smoother.

The same is true for uphill challenges I face throughout the day. Because I remain calm, I don't defeat my own efforts to get all that I have to do done and have it done on time. I have a God-centered poise that keeps my mind free of distress, whether I'm planning ahead or on the spur of the moment.

Throughout all kinds of challenges, I remain poised and in control. As I concentrate on keeping my thoughts and my life centered on the presence of God, I am serene. I am ready to take on the day, anticipating that good is waiting for me.

In all situations, I have a God-centered poise
that keeps me calm and serene.

Daily Word for Teens

New World

*"If you know exactly where you are going . . . and exactly
what you will see along the way, it is not an adventure. . . . It is
also only from adventures and their newness that we learn."
—M. Scott Peck*

As a newborn, my first view of the world was surely
through eyes of wonder. The sights, sounds, and smells
around me must have delighted my senses, because the
world was a new place to me.

Of course, now I'm comfortable and used to my
surroundings most of the time, but occasionally I still find
myself in a new situation that feels like a whole new
world. Maybe it's a new school or a new job. Maybe
there has been a change in my family structure, such as
my going to live with a different parent or adjusting to
having a new brother, sister, or step-parent. Suddenly I
feel like an explorer in a vast new territory. I have so
much to learn: where everything is, how to get along
with the people here, and what is expected of me in this
new scene.

There are challenges to overcome—that's for sure—
but a new world also offers me delightful new discoveries
and blessings. I am ready to explore!

*I am ready to explore, to learn, and to receive
the blessings waiting for me in every new situation.*

HIGHEST AND BEST

—◆—

*"The Law of Win/Win says, 'Let's not do it your way
or my way; let's do it the best way.'"*
—*Greg Anderson*

What works best for everyone else can be a blessing
for me, too. So, when I pray, I ask God for an outcome
that will be best for everyone, not just for myself. I am
glad that I don't need to know what the answer is,
because it would probably be complicated to figure out
on my own! But God knows the answer that will bless
each and every person involved.

Relying on God's answer in resolving all conflict, I
don't push for my own needs to be served. Others may
cooperate even more when they realize that I am am
being considerate of them and not out to get what *I* want!

God loves us all equally, so I know that the divine
solution will be one that is loving to everyone. I turn the
problem over to God in prayer, affirming that every
person in the situation will be blessed by the outcome.
Trusting in God, I am sure that a divine solution is
unfolding.

*I pray for the highest and best for everyone, trusting
that all will be blessed by a divine solution.*

Daily Word for Teens

Co-Creator

"There is no limit to what you can do or be if you have the courage to launch out into the depth of spiritual thinking."
—*Eric Butterworth*

Rather than thinking that I can sit back and wait for good things to happen, I understand that God created me with a mind that I can use to look into all kinds of possibilities and figure out how to make them a reality. As I do this, I am being a co-creator with God in creating good.

But first I pray, asking for guidance. The answer may be a nudge forward in a plan to which I say, "Yes, this is what I need to do and want to do. This is an idea that has merit. This is a plan that opens up a whole world of possibilities."

As a co-creator with God, I bless my body by maintaining healthful routines and eating habits. I bless my mind by using it, taking classes and pursuing my special interests by joining clubs, reading books, and surfing the Internet. I bless my spirit by being aware of God and by cooperating with God in a divine plan of good.

*I am a co-creator with God
in creating my good.*

Daily Word for Teens

MEDITATION

Answers

◆

Doing my homework, I may fantasize about how great it would be to have the answers to every question right in front of me. I know that, in the long run, it would not benefit me to have the answers handed to me. At some point in time, I'm probably going to have to know the information on my own, whether it's on the next test or in real life.

I don't have all the answers to life either, but as I close my eyes and turn within to God, I feel God's presence surrounding me and lifting what might seem like the weight of the world off my shoulders. Now I realize that it's okay that I don't have all the answers, because I realize that God does.

God knows every question of my heart and soul, and all I have to do is to be still and listen for the answers I am seeking. God tells me everything that I need to know. Because I have God, I have the answers to life's questions as I need them.

God provides the answer to every question
of my heart and soul.

I WISH

If a genie granted me three wishes,
I would choose:

_____

_____

_____

_____

_____

_____

_____

_____

_____

_____

_____

Daily Word for Teens

LET GO AND LET GOD

—◆—

"Our prayers should be for blessings in general,
for God knows best what is good for us."
—Socrates

When I was little, I might have made a birthday wish list for my parents or grandparents, or dropped hints about that certain toy I just had to have. Now that I'm older, I sometimes give God a wish list of exactly what I think is best for my life. But I know an even better way: I open my mind to God's plan—which could be something even greater than what I was imagining.

It can be hard at first to let go of what I think should happen, but when I do, it is all so easy. Suddenly I don't have to be in charge anymore. What a good feeling that is! God does bring about the right answer to my prayers, and even though it isn't always what I expected, it is always the best outcome for me.

God works miracles all the time, and I am ready to let go and let God work a miracle in my life right now. Giving every concern to God, I am thankful that the answer is there.

I let go and let God take care of the answer
to my prayers.

ONE PRESENCE, ONE POWER

---◆---

"There is one body and one Spirit . . . one God and Father of all,
who is above all and through all and in all."
—Ephesians 4:4–6

There is one true presence and power in all life, and that is God. God is everywhere present: inside me, all around me, and within everyone and everything. When I am afraid, it is because I am mistakenly imagining that there is something in the world that can have more power than God. And in truth, there is nothing in the world that is stronger than the awesome, loving power of God.

People may have done or said unkind or unloving things to me, but they do not have the power to take away my joy. The only power that I recognize as having dominion over me and my life is God. Whenever I feel uncertain or afraid, I give my full attention to the loving, healing, comforting presence of God that is within me and all around me. I acknowledge no other power than God. I call on the power of God to protect me, and the presence of God to watch over me. I know that all is well.

God is the one presence and one power
in my life.

PET BLESSING

—◆—

"God made the wild animals of the earth of every kind, and the cattle of every kind, and everything that creeps upon the ground of every kind. And God saw that it was good."
—Genesis 1:25

Pets are special beings. They are great at giving love unconditionally. Dogs love to greet their human friends when they come home. Cats purr in any lap they can find. Even hamsters fascinate their owners with their cute and silly antics. My own pet or a favorite pet that belongs to a friend can bring a smile to my face on even those really challenging days.

Right now, I think of all the wonderful furry or feathery friends who are so willing to give their love. I think of the ones who are homeless as well as those who have a human family to love them. I send a prayer to all of God's creatures who so willingly give their love:

"God, bless my pet and all pets. May they all have homes with people who care for them as the precious beings they are, and may they be healthy and happy and loved every day by the people they so freely love. Amen."

I bless all of God's wonderful creatures in prayer, giving thanks for their unconditional love.

INSPIRATION

—◆—

"Genius is one percent inspiration
and ninety-nine percent perspiration."
—Thomas Edison

I know inspiration as ideas that come from God, but it's up to me to follow through by taking action on those ideas. I look for opportunities to use my talents, my enthusiasm, and my energy in ways that fulfill me and help others.

Do I want to be a teacher? Then, even while I'm preparing for that through school and study, I can be involved in the lives of children in positive ways—as a babysitter, Sunday school teacher, or after-school caregiver.

Am I interested in being a lawyer? Joining a debate team now, learning good study habits, and taking an interest in world events can help me prepare for a career in law. If I am inspired to compete in a future Olympic event, then I work toward that goal, giving my best and bringing out the best in myself now.

There is no limit to what I can do when I act on the inspiration of God.

God inspires me to be a creative, caring,
and dynamic person right now.

Daily Word for Teens

I Am a Miracle!

*"[The body is] a marvelous machine, a chemical laboratory,
a power-house. Every movement, voluntary or involuntary,
full of secrets and marvels!"*
—Theodor Herzl

Okay, I will say this slowly and quietly to myself: "I am a miracle." That declaration may cause me to laugh at first and question, "I am a miracle? Me?"

But by the second or third time I say, "I am a miracle," I speak with greater conviction. I feel a confirmation of this truth within me. It's as if the very cells of my body are saying, "Yes, you've got it right!"

I have been designed by God to be a living, breathing miracle of life. When I think about the simplest things that require the cooperation of my spirit, mind, and body, I am amazed. For instance, sitting with my family at home or with friends in the lunch room, I can think and eat, talk and listen. I give and receive from a heart of love. I laugh and cry over what I am feeling about myself and also what I am feeling for others.

Yes, I am a miracle. I also accept that every person on Earth is a miracle. This is a miracle-filled world!

I am a living, breathing miracle of life!

DIVERSITY

— ◆ —

*"We all live with the objective of being happy;
our lives are all different and yet the same."*
—Anne Frank

When I have a chance to meet people from different areas of my country or the world and learn about their beliefs, traditions, and cultures, I have respect for the diversity within the world. I also appreciate that my own beliefs, traditions, and culture add to that diversity.

Life, all life, is a gift from God. I thank God for diversity. If all people looked, thought, and acted exactly alike, life would be boring. But it's not; life is interesting, exciting, and extraordinary.

Today and every day there is the possibility of my meeting people who will offer me a variety of life experiences, observations, and styles. These people each differ in their own way because they are each a one-of-a-kind creation of God.

I accept people for who they are and I respect their beliefs. I embrace and give thanks for the diversity of all life.

Thank You, God, for diversity!

MEDITATION
Breathe and Smile

◆

In this here-and-now moment, I take a mini-vacation. Setting aside the things I need to do, I let my body relax. I close my eyes and count slowly backward from ten to one, breathing deeply and calmly.

I imagine that I am lying in a sailboat on a calm lake. I become more and more aware of the sensation of being slowly rocked by the gently lapping waves and of feeling the warm sun on my skin, until this imaginary setting is as real to me as any other.

There is nothing to do here—no chores, no homework—just me, the sun, the waves, and a light breeze that caresses my cares away. I don't need to do anything except to breathe and smile, taking in this peaceful experience.

I feel refreshed as I return to my day renewed in body, mind, and soul, knowing that I can take a mini-vacation whenever I wish.

I set aside my cares as I enjoy a peaceful visit to an imaginary retreat.

ADMIRABLE ME

What do I think my friends
most admire about me?

_____

_____

_____

_____

_____

_____

_____

_____

_____

_____

_____

_____

BEING ME!

BY RAQUEL

I was born and raised in poverty. My dad was an alcoholic who isolated himself in his room most of the time. My mom worked but could never pay all the bills. Mom would come home from work late and leave early in the morning, so my two younger brothers and I never really saw much of her. By the time I was eight years old, I was "Mom" to my brothers, making sure they did their homework and had food to eat.

I had a major self-esteem issue. Because I thought of myself as ugly and fat, I was always putting myself down, but every morning my mother would wake me up by saying, "Good morning, beautiful!" Mom always gave me encouragement through her words and through her smile.

My parents were legally married for sixteen years. Though I felt that the marriage ended when I was very young, they divorced only a year ago. My dad moved out and into his own apartment when I was nine years old. One of my brothers and I stayed with Dad that summer, but I moved back with Mom when school started—back to moving from one messy apartment to another, because we couldn't pay the rent. We moved about fifteen times by the time I was fourteen years old.

My biggest fear was that my brothers and I would be taken away from both our parents and put in separate foster homes. But about two years ago, my dad started trying to sober up. He has actually slipped a couple of times, and it has been three months since the very last time he messed up. That may not seem like a long time or a big deal, but for someone who had been drunk for 31 years of his life it is, and I am very proud of him.

I have a very positive attitude. I try to be happy and keep a smile on my face, because my mom always smiles. I appreciate that about her, and I also appreciate that she always gives me love, even though she hasn't always been able to take care of me.

Last year my mom dropped my brothers and me off at my dad's place, saying, "I'll be back in a couple of weeks to pick you up." We've been staying with my dad ever since; I guess Mom never found a place for all of us to live.

The good news is that Dad has been taking care of us. He has actually built up his own business. We live in the best part of town, we go to state-recognized schools, and our grades are great. My brothers and I have bank accounts, and I have invested in stocks with some of the money I earned from babysitting. I also paid for my trip to see my best friend in Maine.

Prayer was the only thing that got me through it all. I learned how to pray when I started attending a Unity church when I was about eight years old. I listened to the minister pray in a positive way that helped me stay positive. I've always been told that I was mature for my age. I believe this is because I was interested in listening to adults. I kind of picked up a maturity from paying attention to older people in my life.

I was voted spiritual leader of my preteen church program. That was so cool—sharing my relationship with God in a group.

Then I graduated into the group for teens. Everyone accepts me. There have been times when I would come to church feeling sad, but I could not help but leave feeling happy, because everyone there loves unconditionally. The teens and leaders make me feel so good about myself, and being a part of the group gives me a reason to keep going.

I am interested in theater. It may be something I pursue, but I also know that the chance of me getting a permanent job in theater is slim. So I am leaving myself open to other options.

I have learned a lot from both my mom and dad—how to be and how not to be. Yet I believe if I had missed out on any of what I have experienced, I would not be who I am today. And I like being me!

OPEN MIND

— ◆ —

"If you open your heart, love opens your mind."
—Lowen & Navarro

There are many loving, life-affirming, positive ideas being shared in the world. By keeping an open mind, I allow myself to at least consider new ideas. When I hear others express opinions that I don't understand or agree with, I don't automatically deny that what they have shared is of value. I consider the opinions of others and ask questions to help me understand their viewpoints. They may be able to see an angle of a situation that I haven't thought of yet, or perhaps they simply know more about it than I do.

Of course, I have my own opinions and beliefs, and I honor them, too. I don't accept ideas that are not loving and respectful of other people. I seek out life-affirming, positive people and ideas. When I hear something that I don't agree with 100 percent, I accept what I can use according to my beliefs, and I discard the rest. I enrich my life by being receptive to new ideas and new ways of looking at life.

I keep an open mind to the loving, life-affirming,
positive ideas in God's world.

TODAY

"This is the day that the Lord has made;
let us rejoice and be glad in it."
—Psalms 118:24

Today and every day is special, because it is a day that God is giving me to enjoy life and to bring joy to life. Do I have a test today? Well, then, this is an opportunity for me to show how much I know on the subject and also how much more I need to learn about it.

Is this the day I try to fix a relationship that has an out-of-order sign hanging on it? I know that it will take both the other person and me working together to get our relationship up and going again, but I am willing to try.

When I think of each day as a time that God is giving me to experience and to express the wonder of life, I am eager to do just that. Putting no limits on the good I will experience and express today, I am offered an amazing panorama to explore. I may surprise others and even myself with all that I can contribute to this day and receive from it.

Today is a day in which I experience
and express the wonder of God.

Cosmic Connection

"Ever since the creation of the world his eternal power and divine nature, invisible though they are, have been understood and seen through the things he has made."
—Romans 1:20

Looking up at stars at night from a remote place, far from the lights of a city, I may feel as if I could reach up and pluck a brilliant star from the sky. I feel in touch with and connected to the universe. I experience a cosmic connection—a unity with God and with God's universe.

Because everything has been created by God, there is no denying that I, too, am a creation of the Master Creator. I live and breathe as a divine being. The same elements that the stars and the entire universe are made of are the building blocks for the cells in my body. The same life force that created the stars and causes them to twinkle overhead also gave me life and recharges me with life every day.

I may feel lonely at times, but I am never alone. I am always joined with God and with all life in a cosmic connection, a network of life and creation that extends to the farthest star.

I am one with God and with a universe of God's creation.

Daily Word for Teens

THE POWER OF ONE

—◆—

"Be sure you put your feet in the right place,
then stand firm."
—Abraham Lincoln

If I ever thought for one moment that I couldn't make a difference in the world because I am just one person, I immediately erase such an untrue, unproductive thought from my mind. I *do* make a difference, because I understand that there is great power in just one person, when that one person is living a life grounded in the presence of God. I am just one—but one who has the power of God within me and available to me all the time.

"God, thank You for showing me that by choosing my words wisely, I inspire others with positive, life-affirming ideas. Thank You for guiding my hands so that I create something of beauty and worth for the world to enjoy. Thank You for bolstering my spirits so that when I face an obstacle, I step forward in faith and I persevere. Thank You, God, for Your power within that allows me to make positive changes in my life and in the lives of others."

I have the power to make a positive difference, because
the power of God is within me.

ANGELS AMONG US

◆

"There are angels among us . . . They come to you and me
in our darkest hours to show us how to live, to teach us
how to give, to guide us with the light of love."
—Becky Hobbs and Don Goodman

The theme of angels is everywhere: There are books,
TV shows, and magazine stories about them. There seem
to be so many kinds of angels—celestial beings with
powerful wings in paintings or as sculptures, human
beings who as ordinary people have done extraordinary
things, and intuitive ideas that offer divine guidance.

The world defines angels in many different ways, but
to me, angels represent divine assistance. I know that
God helps me and guides me in many ways—through the
kindness of others, through messages of inspiration that I
hear in meditation, and through intuition, that gentle
voice within that tells me the right thing to do.

Whether I see an angel in a painting, as a person, or as
a divine idea, I let it be a reminder that God is right here
with me and that divine help is always available to me.

Divine assistance helps me and guides me
along my way.

My Own Path

—◆—

"I love my mother. . . . it must have been the most difficult part of mothering: knowing the outcome, yet feeling she had no right to keep me from charting my own path. . . . never once having said, 'I told you so.'"—Erma Bombeck

When I was a child, the hallway just outside my own room might have seemed a scary path at night. And my first day at school was an adventure into the unknown. Those are just two of many paths that at first made me feel unsure of myself and where I was going. But in time they became familiar and friendly ways for me.

When it's time for life after high school, I will step onto a whole new path and accept new responsibilities for myself. It's my own path, leading me to my future. I might blaze my own trail, not following in the footsteps of my parents or siblings by attending the same college or pursuing the same interests.

I appreciate those who support me in following the call of Spirit within me to be myself, and I honor that call by choosing my own path, the one on which I express those sacred qualities that God has given me to express.

I answer the call of Spirit to follow my own path.

MEDITATION

Family Harmony

◆

As I spend some time quietly meditating with God, I reflect about my family. Feeling calm and at ease, it is easy for me to see them in the most loving light.

I visualize my parents as they were growing up. I think about what I know about their early years, and I realize that they have probably gone through many of the same experiences that I have. I see them now as parents who treat me with an understanding that comes from remembering what it was like to be a teen.

I picture my siblings in the light of love, also. Even though there are many experiences that are unique to each of us, we too have experienced some of the same situations in life and have a lot in common.

Most of all, I picture my family and me living in harmony, sharing the good times and the challenging times in love and mutual respect. I see us as always aware that we are God's family, a family living together in harmony and love.

My family and I live together as God's family
of harmony and love.

GOOD NEWS

I see negative stuff in the news all the time.
I can make good things happen in my world when I:

_____

_____

_____

_____

_____

_____

_____

_____

_____

_____

_____

ONE THOUGHT AT A TIME

---◆---

*"Bless a thing and it will bless you. . . . If you bless a situation,
it has no power to hurt you, and even if it is troublesome
for a time, it will gradually fade out, if you sincerely bless it."*
—Emmet Fox

It might feel like I have a million things on my mind at one time, with classes, after-school activities, and chores at home. But I can only think of one thing at a time! And my thoughts are the raw material that shape my reality every day. My positive thoughts form tomorrow's positive outcomes.

Knowing this simple truth, I ask myself often, "What am I thinking right now?" Is it a loving, hopeful thought? I can certainly manage one thought at a time, and in fact, that is all I can do. So I put a positive frame around every situation that comes to mind. If I am feeling upset about a relationship, I bless it with the light of God's love and say a little prayer.

My next thought might be of something I had forgotten to do: my homework! I don't panic, because I immediately affirm: *I have all of God's wisdom to help me get my work done on time.* I think good thoughts, and as I do, I help create good in my own life!

*With one positive thought at a time,
I create good in my life.*

GRACE

"Grace is God's gift of love and mercy, given freely to us whether or not we deserve it. We cannot steal, borrow, buy, or earn it. We can only accept or refuse it."
—Hypatia Hasbrouck

Grace is God's unconditional love for me. There is nothing I can do to earn it or deserve it; it is mine as a gift from God, and I accept it.

I experience grace as both expected and unexpected blessings. Just when I think life is as good as it gets, it gets even better. Of course there are those bumps in the road that wake me when I seem to be asleep at the wheel of my life. It's as if God is giving me a gentle nudge to help me stay alert, on track, and moving in the right direction.

No matter how many mistakes I've made, God loves me! No matter what things I've done that I regret, God loves me! God's grace means that I always have another chance to get it right. No matter how undeserving I feel for any reason, God is always loving me, accepting me, and giving me another chance to learn and grow through the divine gift of grace.

God's grace is the love of my creator
that is continually blessing me.

I CAN!
---◆---

*"If you think you can do a thing
or think you can't do a thing, you're right."*
—Henry Ford

I've heard it said that attitude is everything. I have discovered that in many ways this is true. The difference between my succeeding or not often depends on whether I *believe* I will succeed. If I start out thinking that I can't do something, I might not even bother trying, and not trying is a silly reason to fail!

I won't listen to anyone who tries to tell me that I don't have the ability to do something. When I hear that opinion, I consider it motivation to prove that I can. After all, no one knows me as well as I know myself! Besides, I have the power of God to help me with whatever I need to achieve.

The first step in my success is knowing "I can!" When I believe in myself, I try. And when I try, believing I can succeed, I won't give up. I give it my all. When I'm giving my all, I am much more likely to make it to the finish line—maybe even in first place!

*As my first step in every goal I undertake, I affirm:
"I can!"*

MEMORIES

---◆---

*"History, although sometimes made up of the few acts of
the great, is more often shaped by the many acts of the small."*
—Mark Twain

Recalling happy times—memories of people and events
that have blessed me—I take an imaginary trip in a time
machine. Going back in time to these special moments
stirs up feelings of happiness within me each time I think
about them and the people I shared them with.

What I am recognizing more and more is that each day
I help create joyful memories for all my tomorrows. My
positive attitude today inspires me to think and speak and
act in ways that contribute to memories that I will
treasure in the future.

I don't always decide what will happen each day, but I
do decide how I choose to respond to each day's events.
By what I think, do, and say, I have the power to create
joyful, lasting memories. Even in the toughest of times, I
feel good when I remember the joys of my yesterdays
and know that each new day's joy adds to the joy of my
tomorrows.

*My positive thoughts, words, and actions of today
are creating joyful memories for tomorrow.*

Daily Word for Teens

PRODUCTIVE LIFE

——— ◆ ———

"You yourself, as much as anybody in the entire universe, deserve your love and affection."
—Buddha

Living a productive life means different things to different people. To some it might mean accomplishing financial goals. To others it might be a measure of how much they can get done in a single day.

But what does it mean to me? I know that it's not about how much I accumulate or how much I accomplish. It's about who I am and how I share myself with others. And who am I? I am a child of God, and I am precious to God. Because I know who I am, living a productive life means that I naturally share the love of God with my family, my friends, my community, and my environment in countless ways, in everything I do.

I am content with who I am, so I don't seek happiness from outside sources. With God's love surrounding me, I feel fulfilled because I am leading a productive life of sharing that love with others.

*I am happy and fulfilled
as I share the love of God with others.*

ADVENTURE

◆

*"Far away in the sunshine are my highest aspirations.
I may not reach them, but I can look up and see their beauty,
believe in them, and try to follow where they lead."*
—Louisa May Alcott

An adventure might be many things for me: It might be daring to be different than my friends or members of my family by having my own particular goals, style, and opinions.

With great determination, I might work at trying to accomplish something such as a career in music when others tell me I don't have a chance of making the grade. Just maybe I will be the first in my family to go off to college and earn a degree.

Whatever adventure I choose, it will be right for me because I rely on God for direction. Ever so gently, God assures me that being different is natural for me because I am not made from a mold; I am a one-of-a-kind creation.

I can be a trendsetter or a role model when I am doing something that I truly believe in and that fulfills me. Life itself is an adventure, and I look forward to living it as the wise and capable person that I am.

*I rely on God for the inspiration to choose and participate
in my own adventures in life.*

MEDITATION
Pray In

◆

Before I enter school each day, attend a social event, or begin anything that is important to me, I "pray in." Taking a few moments to be alone with God, I become still. I quiet my thoughts, and I pray words like these:

"God, thank you for this day and for the love and light that are within me and everyone I meet. Help me to see the good in everyone, including myself, and in every situation. Let me always be quick to forgive and eager to understand. Give me words to say that will help, heal, inspire, and comfort. Show me the lessons that You would have me learn today, and teach me to be loving. Remind me that You are walking with me and guiding me on my path, every step of the way. Reveal the joyful moments You have prepared for me today.

"I am open to Your blessings in this day, God. Amen."

*I offer a heartfelt prayer to God as a prelude
to every important event in my life.*

QUALITY PEOPLE

I hang out with people I can respect.
The qualities I look for in a friend are:

_____

_____

_____

_____

_____

_____

The qualities I look for in a date are:

_____

_____

_____

_____

_____

_____

THE IMPORTANCE OF FRIENDSHIP

BY LINC

As a kid in grade school, I wasn't really sure why my parents were getting a divorce. I knew they argued—so much that I actually felt relieved after the divorce, because I no longer had to listen to their constant arguments. After the divorce, I divided my time between two homes: my dad's and my mom's. That was a challenge at times, but the atmosphere in both homes was a lot less tense.

Some of my friends were not so lucky. Their parents divorced at about the same time or a little after mine did. I watched how these kids tried to cope after their parents divorced. There are so many different emotions that kids go through when a family breaks up. Not all, but some younger kids are so confused that they believe the breakup is somehow their fault, and they carry around such a heavy feeling of guilt. I believe that the best thing these kids can do is just try to realize it's not their fault. Although it's not as easy as it sounds, they need to just be there for both parents and not blame themselves or their parents.

That is really hard to do in some cases, because moms and dads may feed their side of the story to their kids, trying to win them over. Some of my friends were caught

Daily Word for Teens

up in this kind of struggle; they were pawns as first one parent and then the other used them to get back at each other. This kind of game was a no-win situation and really tough on my friends. Talking with one another about what we were going through helped. I realized how much I appreciated my mom and dad, because they never did anything that made me think I should or would have to choose one of them over the other.

My dad and I were best friends and still are. So I spent most of my time with my dad. I had friends in my mom's neighborhood and also in my dad's. I never tired of being with my friends, because I was always moving back and forth between my parents' places.

Sometimes, when I was very young, I would get mad at my dad—for an hour or so I would think I loved my mom more. And the opposite happened when I was upset with my mom. But I could never stay mad or upset with either one of them for very long.

Prayer has always been a part of my life. I have to admit, I haven't gone to church every Sunday of my life, but my grandparents and my mom took me whenever I was with them. Later I would go to church with my friends. So prayer and church were a solid foundation for me to grow on and helped me to cope with whatever I was going through.

Although my parents' marriage didn't last, I believe in marriage and hope to marry someday. When I finally decide to get married, and that's not anytime soon, I want to be at a place in my life where I can settle down, relax, and enjoy my family, because that's what life is all about.

I want to be able to sit down with my wife—nothing special planned or happening—and the two of us talk about everything and nothing. We might talk about how much the grass in our yard has grown or how our kids are doing in school. We might just talk and laugh and carry on like kids ourselves. Why should we let ourselves be so serious just because we are grown-ups?

I want the person I marry to be my friend, someone I can have a good time with whether we are walking to the grocery store, going to the movies, or going out on a special occasion. Love is important between any married couple, but I believe that friendship is just as important. That someone special I love I also want as my friend—that's the kind of person I want to spend my life with.

COMFORT ZONE

◆

*"Be like the turtle. If he didn't stick his neck out,
he wouldn't get anywhere at all."*
—Harvey Mackay

Everybody likes to be comfortable. I feel really comfortable staying with my routine and not trying new things, but that makes my day pretty boring. And I certainly would limit my range of experiences!

There are things that I really want to do, but that make me break out in a cold sweat just thinking about them! The list might include public speaking, jumping off a high-dive platform, trying out for a sports team, or even telling someone "I love you!" But I do have to take some risks if I want to really enjoy life.

So I take a deep breath as I step out of my comfort zone. When I face my fears and move through them by taking action toward my goals, a surprising thing happens: My comfort zone expands! It might take a few tries at something new before I feel really at ease, but gradually I become comfortable in this new activity. The thing I used to fear now adds an exciting new dimension to my life.

*I am expanding the limits of my comfort zone
by facing fears and moving through them.*

Daily Word for Teens

CARING FOR OTHERS

—◆—

"Those who bring sunshine to the lives of others
cannot keep it from themselves."
—James Barrie

Taking care of little brothers or sisters or other kids
may not be my favorite thing to do, but having a positive,
fun-loving attitude helps me make our time together
special and fun for us all. I can enjoy being with these
kids as much as they enjoy being with me.

Doing something for my parents or a neighbor to help
lighten their workload gives me an opportunity to learn
about being an adult and especially about being a parent.
I come away from a time of helping them with a greater
respect for them and appreciation for all that they do.

Helping grandparents around the house, I might mow
the lawn, vacuum the carpet, or write a letter for them.
It's great to see the smile of appreciation on their faces
and to hear it directly from them.

In caring for others, I help bridge the generations that
make up my family and my network of friends. It's true:
We do care about and for one another.

Caring for and about others, I help create
special times of sharing among us.

ON MY OWN

◆

"Don't make my mistake, kid.
Don't follow orders your whole life.
Think for yourself."
—Barbatus, in the movie Antz

It's hard to believe, but in a few years, I'll be on my own. Sometimes I can't wait until I can make all of my own decisions without parents or teachers telling me what to do. Other times I'd rather not think about it—it feels a little intimidating to think that it's all going to be up to me!

The good news is that no other person will be telling me what to do, but that doesn't mean I'll be alone in life. After all, I wouldn't even exist without God, and God is always with me. God works through me to help me create my life experience. The more I talk things over with God in prayer as I make decisions, the more I will be led to the experiences that will enrich my life.

I'm sure I will have easy times and difficult times, but I know that God will be right with me, guiding me through it all. On my own, I will think for myself, but I will have the guidance of God supporting me in every decision I make.

As I step out on my own, God supports me
and guides me through every decision I make.

INTEGRITY

— ◆ —

*"Integrity: A name is the blueprint of the thing we call character.
You ask, 'What's in a name?'
I answer, 'Just about everything you do.'"*
—Morris Mandel

The very word "integrity" may sound like a heavy-duty commitment, but it is one that, when I live from it, allows my whole self to contribute something of value. That is an awesome experience!

My true nature is spiritual; I am a spiritual being living through human experiences. I honor God and myself when I am true to the qualities that God has given me to express. So living in the integrity of who I am, I am honest. I don't pretend to be who I'm not or who someone else believes I should be. I am *me*; a creation of God who has a reverence for all life.

When someone—even someone I care for deeply—asks me to do anything that is not in line with the integrity of my soul, I say "no." I do what honors God and what honors others and myself as God's creations. Living from the integrity of my soul lights up my life with meaning and purpose. I feel good being myself and doing what I do.

*Living from the integrity of my soul, I honor God,
myself, and all others.*

CHANGE

◆

"If we don't change, we don't grow.
If we don't grow, we aren't really living."
—Gail Sheehy

I am well aware that I am changing physically.
Sometimes I think I can see changes in myself from one
day to the other: My face may look a bit more like an
adult's, and certainly big changes are going on with my
body. I am growing up!

I may look so much like an adult that my parents and
teachers are expecting much more from me in the way
that I think and act than they did even a few months ago.
That can be frustrating for me, because my physical
growth might be ahead of my emotional growth and the
wisdom that I have gained.

So I rely on God to help me harmonize myself so that I
am making progress physically, mentally, and spiritually.
I need my whole self up and running to cope with the
changes in me and in my life. I am making all kinds of
progress, but some of it might show up better than
others. That's a part of change and what I am adjusting to
in growing up.

I am a whole person who is making progress
physically, mentally, and spiritually.

Daily Word for Teens

TRUST

"I know God will not give me anything I can't handle. I just wish that He didn't trust me so much."
—Mother Teresa

The trust between my parents and me or between my friends and me is a comforting thing, but if one of us makes a mistake and messes up, that bond can become shaky or may disappear all together.

My trust in God, though, can never be shaken. I trust God with each sunrise, knowing that if I don't see the sun in the morning, that's because it is hiding behind the clouds in the sky. Even though I don't see God with my physical eyes, I know God is always there. I trust God to love me unconditionally and without judgment. I trust God to show me the answers I need to know and to provide me with everything I need in life.

Apparently God trusts me, too, because I've been given an awareness of my spiritual nature that means I have a responsibility to act in loving ways. God trusts me to share the abilities I've been given that help make the world a better place, and I trust myself to do just that!

I put my trust in God,
Who is always there for me.

MEDITATION
Faith

◆

My faith is my unquestioning belief that God is
continually blessing me and that there is nothing,
absolutely nothing, beyond God's power to heal.
Because my faith is in God, I know that even
something better than my highest hope is possible.

I visualize how my faith is growing by picturing it
as a tiny seed I have planted in the rich soil of my soul.
As if I am viewing a time-lapse movie, I see my faith-
seed sprouting and then growing taller. New leaves are
forming. Now there is a bud appearing! Next I see
beautiful petals of a flower unfolding. My faith has
grown from a seed to a full bloom!

Faith is a continuing growth process of planting a
faith-seed, nourishing my faith, and knowing that it is
thriving. I keep planting seeds by having faith in God.
I keep my faith alive by nurturing it daily through my
relationship with God. My soul is a beautiful garden
of faith.

*My faith reminds me that something even better
than my highest hope is possible.*

True Confessions

The things I would like to improve
about myself are:

_____

_____

_____

_____

_____

_____

_____

GREAT!
BETTER
GOOD

_____

_____

_____

_____

_____

COMPLETION

---◆---

"The secret of getting ahead is getting started. The secret of getting started is breaking your complex overwhelming tasks into small manageable tasks, and then starting on the first one."
—*Mark Twain*

Why do I procrastinate, putting things off until they seem like such huge tasks? I could buy a book on the subject, but I'd probably put off reading it!

Sometimes I avoid a project because I'm worried I won't be able to do a good job. It's just easier to sit and imagine how great it will turn out, while avoiding my fears of actually doing it! I can help myself get started when I remember that I *can* do it. I can always ask God, family, and friends for help with my commitments.

Breaking the job into small tasks makes it easier, too. I commit to working on the first step for just five minutes. I can stand anything for five minutes! Once I've gotten started, I usually find that I want to keep working.

Keeping a journal of my feelings before and after I complete a task helps me remember that working on a project wasn't nearly as bad as I'd expected it to be, and that finishing it makes me feel great!

I commit to getting started,
and I get the job done!

CHOICES
—◆—

*"The feeling remains that God is
on the journey, too."*
—Teresa of Avila

Every day I make many choices: what I wear, the
music I listen to, the TV shows I watch, and who I spend
my time with. These are simple choices I make on my
own without much trouble.

But what about the really difficult choices I face?
Decisions that affect my life in more long-term ways—
where I'll go to college or whether I'll accept a certain job
offer—can be pretty overwhelming. Sometimes I feel that
I need help to know what to do.

So I turn within and pray. When I pray, I let go of
worries about making the right choice. The presence of
Spirit pours through my mind like a warm, bright light,
and I know I am connecting with the vast intelligence of
God. In this divine light, I can see my options more
clearly. I think of my choices one by one, and when I am
focusing on the right choice for me, a great peace comes
over me. With God's guidance, the answer is clear.

*The light of God illuminates my options
and reveals the right choice to me.*

INNER VOICE

—◆—

"Do you not know that your body is a temple of the Holy Spirit within you, which you have from God?"
—1 Corinthians 6:19

Have I ever thought of my body as a temple of God? Well, it's true. God's spirit is within me, and when I have respect for my own body, my own self, I expect others to respect me also.

As a temple of God's spirit, I might feel, more than hear, a quiet whisper of an inner voice speaking to me, and I listen. This inner voice is always encouraging me, never putting me down. It's as if God is telling me, "I have every confidence in you. Because I have created you, I know what you are capable of doing and being."

There is so much around me competing for my attention that I have to really listen for my inner voice to guide me. Meditation, a time of becoming quiet and connecting consciously with God's spirit, is a perfect time to give my full attention to the good that God is sharing with me. It's a time with God that I enjoy and that also refreshes me.

Listening to that sacred inner voice, I receive the good that God is sharing with me.

A SPECIAL SOMEONE

◆

"Tell me whom you love, and I will tell you who you are."
—Houssaye

There are many people in my life whom I admire, whether they are people I know personally or celebrities. They might be talented, kind, confident, attractive, or funny—and some of them are all of this and more!

When I feel this way about others, I might tend to put them on a pedestal and imagine that they are better than me in some way. But it's hard to be friends if I always feel inferior to others!

Fortunately, I can use my feelings about others to understand myself better. If I'm drawn to someone, it is usually because of qualities he or she possesses that I admire—qualities that *I* have the potential to develop and express more fully. So I silently appreciate them for helping me see the wonderful ways I can express myself. Then I encourage those same qualities in myself. Instead of putting someone on a pedestal, I can become *my own* special someone!

*I am a very special someone who possesses
and expresses admirable qualities.*

Daily Word for Teens

MEETING LIFE

◆

*"And in the end, it's not the years in your life that count.
It's the life in your years."*
—Abraham Lincoln

Although life can be challenging, I meet it with
enthusiasm. I may not know what the future holds for
me, but I do know that every step of the way, God is here
with me.

My motto is: *Carpe diem! Seize the day!* This means that
I embrace all that life has to offer me. I am ready to see
the good in all situations, the loving presence of God in
all people.

Do I have a dream that I would like to fulfill? I do
more than sit and think about it—I seize the moment and
take whatever steps are necessary to begin to fulfill that
dream. I don't let negative thoughts get in my way. With
God helping me, all things are possible!

I live in awareness of God and of the blessing it is just
to be alive in this very moment in time. I accept each day
with open arms, and as I do, I discover the joy and
wonder that each new day brings to me.

*With my arms opened wide,
I meet life enthusiastically.*

WHAT IS A FAMILY?

*"The supreme happiness of life
is the conviction that we are loved."*
—Victor Hugo

How many people does it take to make a family? It can be any number from two to infinity! My family might consist of just me and one parent or grandparent, or several brothers and sisters, or even more than one set of parents!

The important thing about a family is not how many people are in it, but how much love is shared there. I might enjoy loving relationships with my own family at home, but if the situation is less than ideal, I will sometimes feel as though I'm missing out on a really loving environment with adults I can count on.

If that is the case, I can hand-pick a "family of choice" to be my support system. From among the adults I know, I make a mental list of a few special ones whom I really trust and look up to. If I'm an only child, I choose a best friend to be just like a sister or a brother to me. I am grateful to have a family that loves and supports me!

*My family surrounds and supports me
in an environment of love.*

MEDITATION
World Peace

◆

Watching the news or reading about current events, I might question how peace in the world will ever be achieved. Yet I know the answer: Peace happens one heart at a time. So as I meditate in silence, I add to the peace of the world with my own thoughts. I close my eyes in a quiet time and listen as the voice of God reassures me.

I hold thoughts of peace in mind as I imagine all people realizing that there is tremendous power in gentleness. I see everyone in the world showing reverence for one another's sacredness and living together in peace. I picture the leaders of the world truly listening to one another, committed to learning from and respecting other cultures.

As I pray for world peace, I am affirming that through sharing the love of God, the people of all nations are learning to live on planet Earth in fellowship and with understanding.

World peace is becoming a reality—
one heart at a time.

SURE CURE

What helps me most when I'm feeling sad
or when I need some time alone?

_____

_____

_____

_____

_____

_____

_____

_____

_____

_____

_____

_____

Always Time for Prayer

By Kristen

I am from a big family: I have three brothers and three sisters. Right now there are four of us kids living at home with our parents: my brother Josh, who's sixteen; Kristen (that's me and I'm thirteen); my little brother Jacob, who's seven; and my little sister Rachel, who's three.

My two older sisters have their own places. The oldest is married and has a little girl who is now four years old, so by using a little simple math, you know that since I'm thirteen and my niece is four, I became an aunt when I was just nine years old.

My oldest brother Jason died in a car wreck in 1997, and it was a sad time for my family. What helped me was knowing that he went to a better place. It also helped having other family members that I could depend on and who could depend on me.

There are many blessings and also some challenges with having brothers and sisters. The thing that helps me through most of the days is knowing that no matter what I do or no matter what happens, there will always be somebody in the family there for me. And if I have a problem, I go to God, knowing that He will answer my prayers. I

Daily Word for Teens

know that it may not be in the exact way that I want it to be answered, though, and that sometimes I may have to look for the answer. It doesn't usually just pop up.

Since both my mom and dad work, I'm learning there's a lot of responsibilities in being an older child at home. When my parents and older brother Josh are gone, my little brother and sister look to me for answers.

Sometimes it's harder than other times, and I try not to yell at them, but sometimes it just happens, like the time my little brother and sister were running around the house and knocked over this cute little clay dog I had made and it broke.

It was hard to forgive them, but I did. Whenever I get upset with them, I remember how nice my oldest sister was when she would babysit all of us younger kids. I use her as an example of how I should treat them. When my older sister got her car, she would take us places. If we were going somewhere and I needed money, she would loan it to me, and I wouldn't have to pay her back.

Right now I have my own room, so when I need time to myself, I usually just go up there and turn on music and relax for a while. Most days I am so busy with a full schedule, I don't always have time to relax. I may babysit my neighbors' two children from 6:00 A.M. to 7:00 A.M., and then I'm off to school. On Mondays and Wednesdays after school, I have drill-team practice and after that, soccer practice. Then when soccer practice is over, I head home for dinner and to do my homework.

But even with my busy schedule, I find time for prayer, and I go to church on Sundays and a prayer class on Tuesdays. I like it so much I'm going to start attending on Wednesday nights sometimes instead of going to soccer practice. It's a group of seventh- and eighth-grade girls, so we talk about things that are important to us. We understand what one another is going through.

Even more than depending on someone else, though, I know to keep depending on God, because God does answer my prayers. And I keep on remembering that I may have to really look for those answers, but that they are always there.

ENERGY

— ◆ —

"You are never given a wish without also being given the power to make it come true. You may have to work for it, however."
—Richard Bach

There are times when I really need an extra boost of energy for an upcoming sports event or a huge writing assignment, but not even food or rest gives me the energy that I need.

So I become quiet and pray. For a few moments, I linger in the presence of God. Then I feel energy radiating throughout my body. The source of this energy is the spirit of God.

I pray often, so my spiritual battery stays charged. Just a few quiet moments of concentrating on the spirit of God energizes me. After all, God is the source of my life and sustains me with life. Looking to God, I am renewed with a zest for living. A surge of spiritual energy overcomes any physical, mental, and emotional limitations I may have once felt.

I am energized with a vitality and strength of spirit, mind, and body. There is a new me who is full of energy and ready to take on the day.

Full of the energy of life, I am energized
in spirit, mind, and body.

INTUITION

———◆———

*"Listen to your intuition. It will tell you
everything you need to know."*
—Anthony J. D'Angelo

I may be busy watching TV or reading a book, when suddenly I am aware of a strong feeling that is telling me I need to call my best friend.

What I am sensing is not strange; it is spiritual. I have a power of perception that is more accurate than any of my five senses. God has given me intuitive power—an inner knowing of what to do and when to do it to be of the most help.

Yet, it is up to me to be sensitive to the gentle urging, the spontaneity of this wisdom of the heart. The very best advice of others and the longest list of why's and why-not's that I can think my way through don't offer me my best options and actions.

So I act on my intuition and call my best friend. Then I learn how important my call was to her: She needed to talk to someone who would listen and help her through a tough time. Because I acted on my intuition, I was that someone!

*Listening to my intuition, I act
on the wisdom of my heart.*

SPIRITUAL HIGH

◆

*"To see a World in a Grain of Sand; And a Heaven
in a Wild Flower; Hold Infinity in the palm of your hand;
And Eternity in an hour."*
—William Blake

I might know people who seem to be trying to find deeper meaning in their lives by experimenting with mind-altering substances. I hear about people who have gotten sick or died from an overdose or an accident while driving under the influence of an illegal substance. But other people I know seem to get away with it—at least so far. They act as if it's all in fun, and they pressure others to go along with them.

I know that by not doing drugs or alcohol, I'm not missing a thing. By meditating at a really deep level, I know what it's like to have an awesome spiritual experience. Immersed in the love of God, I feel a high that no drug can produce, because it's no illusion—it's real. I am super-alert and aware, yet incredibly calm, and the beauty of life amazes me.

My friends might not get it at first, but when they see how mellow I am when I meditate, they might want to know how they, too, can get *spiritually* high.

*Through meditation I experience a spiritual high.
Calm and aware, I am amazed by the beauty of life.*

STRENGTH

---◆---

*"When Jesus heard him, he was amazed and said
to those who followed him, 'Truly I tell you, in no one
in Israel have I found such faith.'"*
—Matthew 8:10

If I'm suddenly in an embarrassing situation, I may
wonder how I'm going to get out of it and save face at
the same time. If someone should snicker or laugh at me,
I try to see the humor in what has happened and laugh
about it, too, rather than reacting in anger. Doing so takes
great spiritual strength.

I have this strength within me all the time, so I know
that I have what it takes to overcome any embarrassing
moments, to adapt to situations, and to learn what I need
to learn to succeed in life. Spiritual strength comes from
knowing that God is always available to me. Strength that
comes from God is far greater than my own or any other
person's could possibly be.

The greatest strength I have is not from my developing
my muscles; it is from expressing God's spirit within me.
I draw confidence from knowing that I have spiritual
strength!

*I have strength of spirit
through the presence of God within me.*

Daily Word for Teens

MOVING

—◆—

"Conquering any difficulty always gives one a secret joy, for it means pushing back a boundary-line and adding to one's liberty."
—Henri Frédéric Amiel

If I could live anywhere in the world, what place would I choose? Would it be a big city teeming with activity and cultural events? Or would I choose a country scene with animals and plants everywhere?

After a lot of consideration, I think I would choose home, which is a feeling about my family, myself, and my friends more than a place. And this attitude of home helps me when I do have to move away from familiar places and people. I might not have a choice about making a move, but I can choose to make it as positive an experience as I can.

Moving often, I might feel that I haven't had time to really adjust or to enjoy the new friends that I have made. Still, when I move on, I take with me good feelings and memories of the times that we shared. Each move gives me an opportunity to form new friendships, to explore new territory, and to know that wherever I am, I am at home in God's world.

Wherever I am, I am at home in God's world.

TALENTS AND ABILITIES

——◆——

"God's gifts put man's best dreams to shame."
—Elizabeth Barrett Browning

I've heard it said that every person has natural talents and abilities—it's just a matter of finding them. It's too bad I can't just look into a crystal ball or crack open a fortune cookie to find out what my talents and abilities are, but I can listen to God's guidance within me as I am led to discovering more about myself and what I am capable of achieving.

I learn to use whatever talents I have to the best of my ability. I may not be the absolute best at what I am doing, but how drab the world would be if only the brightest-colored flowers bloomed or how quiet it would seem if only those birds with the prettiest songs were to sing!

I am discovering the talents and abilities that are God's gifts to me. With every new thing I try, I am open to the possibility of discovering a new and hidden talent—the gift of an ability from God that I can use to better myself and better the world.

Each day I can discover more about myself
and my talents and abilities.

MEDITATION

Loving Myself

◆

It isn't always easy to love everyone, and sometimes it seems hardest just to love myself. And the truth is that if I can learn to love and accept myself, I will find that loving others is easy. Love and acceptance of myself and others may take time, so I practice often.

In a quiet place, I imagine how God must feel about me. I am God's beloved creation! God doesn't withhold love from me because of the faults or mistakes or imperfections that I see in myself. God simply loves me with tenderness and total acceptance.

In meditation, I practice seeing myself as God sees me, the way loving parents accept their children. I affirm: *I am loved and lovable. I am worthy of God's love, and I love myself, just the way I am.* I imagine treating myself with the same kindness, gentleness, and love that I know God offers me and that I would extend to a dear friend.

I am worthy of God's love,
and I love myself, just the way I am.

Daily Word for Teens

MY HEROES

The people I see as my role models
and heroes are:

_____

_____

_____

_____

_____

_____

_____

_____

_____

_____

_____

_____

_____

_____

HANGING OUT

—◆—

*"I believe nobody makes it alone . . . always keep in mind
your relationships. Nurture them, build them,
and lean on them when you need to."*
—Stedman Graham

Here are some hard questions that I ask myself: Am I
happy with the people I call friends? Do I feel good about
myself when I'm around them? Can I respect the things
they do and say? Or am I just spending time with them
because they're the first people I happened to meet in
class or on the team?

Sometimes I need to make a tough decision about
someone I've been spending my time with. If one
person—or even a whole group—I am hanging out with
is doing things that don't meet my moral standards, it's
time for me to move on. I can politely explain my
reasons, but I don't have to if I don't want to. I can just
choose to be busy doing other things with other people.
Eventually the message will be clear that I'm not
interested.

I create a lifelong mutual support system by being part
of a network of quality friendships. So when I find true
friends, I hold on to them!

*I choose to be part of a network of friends
whose activities and morals I respect.*

Daily Word for Teens

TAKING CARE OF MYSELF

◆

*"I realize the importance of exercising the various dimensions
of my body, soul, mind and heart. Taken together,
these aspects give me a sense of wholeness."*
—Robert Fulghum

In a physical education class or at a fitness center, I
give my body a workout. Running or swimming, I
increase my endurance. Stretching my muscles a little
more every day, I become more flexible. Training with
weights, I build muscles. I invest time in taking care of
my body, and I am rewarded with lots of energy and a
good feeling about myself.

I take care of myself spiritually by taking time to be
alone with God every day. I give all challenges to God for
a divine solution, and my faith grows stronger with every
challenge God and I overcome together.

With practice, I am learning to meditate—to be still
and listen to God—for longer periods of time without
being distracted by anyone or anything. Turning within to
God, I turn away from whatever or whomever is causing
me to feel stress and strain. Then I simply linger in the
atmosphere that my peace-filled soul provides for me.

*Taking care of myself—physically and spiritually—
I truly enjoy life!*

HEALING FROM WITHIN

—◆—

*"For I will restore health to you,
and your wounds I will heal."*
—Jeremiah 30:17

When a person I trust has done something that has
hurt me—even to the point of physical or emotional
abuse—I may have a lot of confusing feelings. I might
even mistakenly feel as if it was somehow my fault.

I begin to heal by keeping myself centered in the
presence of God—the very source of healing love that is
within me—and I am strengthened and renewed. I
encourage myself and cooperate with the healing that is
taking place by knowing and affirming: *I am enfolded in
God's healing love.* Softly repeating this to myself helps me
to understand that I am not to blame for the words and
actions of others. Loved by God, I have the courage I
need to go forward.

Every day, in quiet times of prayer and meditation, I
allow myself to feel the healing energy that is always
flowing freely in and through me. I affirm what I know in
my heart is true: *Emotionally, physically, and spiritually, I am
God's perfect, beloved creation.*

**I am God's perfect creation,
enfolded in God's healing love.**

Daily Word for Teens

BEING A FRIEND

◆

*"A friendship can weather most things and thrive in thin soil;
but it needs a little mulch of letters and phone calls
and small, silly presents every so often—just to save it
from drying out completely."—Pam Brown*

I know how important it is for me to have friends, but
I also know that it is just as important for me to be a
friend. As a friend I give love, understanding, and
straightforward feedback to people I care about. When I
feel that my friends are headed toward trouble or danger,
I speak up and clue them in on what they may not be
consciously thinking is a problem. As much as I value our
friendship, I consider their well-being and safety of more
importance.

Being a friend, I pray for the people who fill important
roles as close companions, classmates, and neighbors. We
are walking together on the path of life for a short time or
maybe a long time. I want them to know that I am a
compassionate, caring, and honest friend who is there for
them in the best of times and what may seem the worst of
times. I remind them and myself that as close as we may
all be, God's spirit within each of us is what unites us.

*I am a compassionate, caring friend who
is always there for my friends.*

Daily Word for Teens

SERVICE

"Everyone needs to be valued.
Everyone has the potential to give something back."
—Diana, Princess of Wales

When someone asks, "Will you do me a favor?" I might say "yes" even before I know what I am being asked to do. I may change that *yes* to a polite *no* when I hear what that favor is, but I am willing to help others for no other reason than the good feelings I receive from being helpful.

I serve God by helping God's family here on Earth. I give good back to God by helping people who need someone to be their feet when they cannot walk, their voices when they cannot speak, and their caregiver when they cannot care for themselves.

Serving others is important to me, and it might even lead me to a career in social work, health care, or counseling. Even if I pursue another career, there will always be opportunities for me to serve others by being helpful, kind, and compassionate. I can satisfy my own desire to be helpful by doing small favors and by helping others make it through the day.

I serve God by helping God's family here on Earth.

TRANSFORMATION

—◆—

"The moment you have in your heart this extraordinary thing called love and feel the depth, the delight, the ecstasy of it, you will discover that for you the world is transformed."
—J. Krishnamurti

I've had days that started out great, and then something happened that caused me and a friend or family member to get into an argument. Trying to talk with the other person just made it worse, and I might have felt as if there was nothing I could do.

But there is something I can do. First, I acknowledge what I'm feeling—hurt or anger or frustration. I write my feelings down in a journal, or I confide in a trusted friend. Then, when I'm ready to let go of my need to prove my point, I find a quiet place to clear my thoughts. I let myself feel the healing power of God's love that is always there in my heart. I let it calm me and soothe my emotions. I imagine love radiating from my heart, through my body, and out toward everyone and everything.

The power of love is amazing. Because I'm willing to let love do its work through me, I feel peaceful again, and my whole day is turned around to good.

Love heals everything.

MEDITATION
Awareness

◆

My awareness is a realization that takes me
beyond what I can see or hear or touch. Turning up
my awareness of God, I now move into a time of
knowing God's presence with my whole being.

Awareness of God works much like a microscope,
because it gives me a view of what is within the outer
layer of my physical form. I see myself as I have
never seen myself before: I am glowing with the light
of God that is radiating from the center of my being. I
bring others into this awareness—one by one I see
the brilliance of God's spirit shining in my friends and
family.

I let this turned-up awareness continue as I go
about my day. I see every person and every situation
in a new light—the light of God. Everyone and
everything seems brighter. I have lightened up also,
because I know that God's spirit is shining brightly in
the world.

Aware of God's presence, I see my world glowing
with God's spirit.

LIFE LESSONS

Some lessons God has been teaching me lately are:

_____

_____

_____

_____

_____

_____

_____

_____

_____

_____

_____

_____

_____

Quitters Do Win

By Louis

L ast summer I was elected regional officer of seven states by my church youth group. It's a youth-led organization—by the youth, for the youth. In it, you connect with people from other states and other parts of the country, and together you become aware of your connection to God. It's amazing, once you realize that God's inside of you.

When I became an officer, I kind of had a spiritual awakening. It's an important leadership role, and I realized that if I was going to be in that role, I needed to give up a habit: I was using drugs—mostly pot.

I had never, ever thought that I had a problem with it. I thought of it as just kind of a recreation thing for me that I did with my friends. When I got high, I thought that I was being spiritual and getting closer to God, and I thought that I was aware of what was going on around me. I didn't see getting high as something that blocked me from reality, because I thought I knew what I was doing when I was high. But once I stopped, I realized that I had been in a fog most of the time. And now that I was an officer with a lot of responsibilities for the coming year, I decided that doing drugs wasn't for me. I realized that if I couldn't see myself as whole and perfect without needing drugs, then there was something wrong there.

I came clean with everyone when I stopped. I talked to

my mom, and then my dad and stepmom. I told them all what I'd been doing: when, where, how—I mean, just everything. I released it all to them. My mom and I have been friends forever, but things are even better now: I'm a lot more open about things with my parents. It was totally amazing that I could be open with them and just let them know what was on my mind. And I think the reason they all took it really, really well was because I did stop doing drugs for myself—not because I got in trouble.

I didn't think it was all going to be easy. But when I quit, all my friends, even the ones that I had been getting high with, were actually really cool and supportive of me instead of condemning me for it as I'd expected. And the neatest thing that came out of all of this is that still today, more of my friends keep looking toward me to help them step out of that circle and quit, too.

Now when I'm around people who are using, I turn my thoughts within and take a deep breath, and I know that using drugs is not where I need to be. I use my spiritual principles as a guide. And I really surround myself with good people. My friends and I are good supports for each other.

Quitting drugs turned out to be the best thing that I've ever done. I'm 18 and really looking forward to the rest of this year as a regional officer, because this year wouldn't have happened in the same way if I hadn't made this choice for myself.

I try to remember, when things seem like they're too much and I'm feeling pressured, to just close my eyes and take a deep breath and think about how much good there is in my life compared to how much bad there is. And so many times, the good tips the scale, and I just smile.

Daily Word for Teens

PRAYED UP

◆

*"And this is my prayer, that your love may overflow
more and more with knowledge and full insight
to help you to determine what is best."*
—Philippians 1:9–10

Every day has its challenges and opportunities, and I
am ready for whatever this day offers me, because I am
prayed up. This means that I pray every day, not just
when I meet a challenge or have an opportunity. Prayer is
as important to me as food and water, rest and exercise.
When I pray, I realize more keenly that God is a power
and presence within me.

Knowing that God is my constant companion and
guide, I don't become stressed out when something
unexpected comes up. When out of the blue, something
happens, my immediate response is this: God and I are
able to handle this together.

And when nothing seems to be happening—at least
nothing I really think needs to happen—I don't feel down
or discouraged. My spirits are refreshed as I talk things
over with God or just stay quiet and let an awareness of
God fill my thoughts so that I think positively and act
with confidence.

*Being prayed up, I have confidence
and I am ready for whatever this day offers me.*

Daily Word for Teens

Slow Down

---◆---

"Learn to enjoy every minute of your life.
Be happy now. . . . Every minute should be enjoyed, savored."
—Earl Nightingale

When I was little, I'm sure I would have enjoyed a story about living in a world made of cookies. If that ever happened, I would not need to eat every cookie at once! I'd slow down and savor each bite, knowing that there would always be more.

And actually, I can compare my life to a never-ending plate of cookies. I have my whole life ahead of me, with countless blessings to discover, so I don't rush. I enjoy every blessing knowing that my blessings will never run out!

There are many blessings awaiting me in adulthood. I might move to a new city on my own, enter into a committed and intimate relationship, or start a family. With God's guidance, I may take these adult steps one day. But for now, I don't let anyone rush me into situations that are best left until I'm older. Right now, I savor every day of my experiences as a teen.

My life holds the promise of unending blessings
waiting to be enjoyed, and I savor each one.

UPS AND DOWNS

"So much of what we know of love we learn at home."
—Unknown

One day my family is getting along and everything is great. The next day everyone is upset and nothing seems to be going right. Being part of a family when things are on the upswing is a real gift from God, but on those down days, I sometimes wish I could be somewhere else.

The truth is, if I weren't so close to the people in my family, it wouldn't matter so much to me if they were angry or upset. But since I love and care deeply for them, it really hurts when I am feeling disconnected from them because of angry or unkind words or actions.

When things are tough in my family, I get in touch with the depth of my feelings. I realize that as strong as my anger and sadness are in that moment, my love for my family is equally powerful. When we are willing to share just a bit of God's healing love, things start looking up again.

*Through all the ups and downs in my family,
there is a constant bond of love that unites us.*

WELL-BEING

———◆———

"You are within God. God is within you."
—*Peace Pilgrim*

I might consider myself to be pretty healthy if I am not running a fever or feeling any discomfort. But whether or not my body is experiencing an illness, there is more to my overall well-being than just my physical condition.

I am a person made up of many layers. On the outside, I am a body that can be seen. Within that body is my mind, where my invisible thoughts and feelings are. Deeper within me is my soul—everlasting, but yet always growing and evolving according to a divine plan. And at the innermost core of me, the pure unchanging spirit of God shines brightly.

I visualize God's spirit within me as a light radiating outward through all the levels of my being: my soul, my mind, my heart, and my body. A gentle, powerful healing energy fills me with a sense of well-being. I know and affirm: *I am well.*

The spirit of God within me is a light that shines healing energy through every level of my being.

WHAT I TREASURE

*"For where your treasure is,
there your heart will be also."*
—Matthew 6:21

My room, my clothes, my CDs—all these are things that I treasure. My taste in and preference for such things may change, because I am changing. Some treasures remain constant: my own God-given qualities and the people who have taught me valuable life lessons by their very example of being courageous, dedicated, and loving.

My greatest treasures are whoever and whatever uplifts my heart and nourishes my soul. Special people and times have made a positive difference in how I view my world and myself. Memories of a vacation or other times when the companionship and laughter of people I loved and who loved me still cause me to smile—days or years later.

What I treasure cannot always be held in my hands, in a box, or on a shelf. What I treasure is in my heart, where I connect with the presence of God within people, events, and the very air I breathe.

*I treasure the loving people and sacred times
that have uplifted my heart and nourished my soul.*

THE FUTURE

◆

*"Our imagination is the only limit
to what we can hope to have in the future."*
—*Charles F. Kettering*

I like thinking about the future, but not at the expense of missing out on enjoying what is happening now. Thinking about my future—what kind of career I will have, whom I will marry, or where I will live is exciting! My imagination kicks into high gear. Will I be a world-class athlete, a Broadway actor, or a college professor? Will I marry someone I know right now or someone I haven't met yet?

I have questions about what will be, but no answers, except for one thing: In the future, I will be in God's loving care—just as I am now. The future is exciting to think about and plan for, that's for sure, but I can get there only one day at a time. I am in no hurry, not when I am enjoying today.

I give thanks for what is yet to be, and I enjoy what is now. I accept and give thanks for the blessings of each day, and I eagerly look forward to the ones that are yet to come.

*Now and always, I am in the loving care
of my Creator.*

Daily Word for Teens

MEDITATION
Right Time

◆

When I am feeling impatient, I want something to happen right now in just the way I want it to happen. Such feelings of restlessness and anxiety let me know that now is the time to take a break. Finding the quietest, most private place I can, I become quiet. I think about the presence of God that is within and around me. I imagine myself being transported to a timeless place—no clocks, calendars, or assignments are competing for my attention.

I feel a gentle presence enfolding me and uplifting me so that I have an overview of what is happening in my life. I see myself moving effortlessly through the days of the coming week. I understand the importance of timing—of everything happening at the right time and in the right order.

Gently returning my awareness to the sights and sounds around me, I am calm and ready to return to the day and the blessings it contains.

Any time is the right time to take a few moments to be uplifted by God's presence.

GOD IS EVERYWHERE

I know that God is all around me.
I see God in:

_____

_____

_____

_____

_____

_____

_____

_____

_____

_____

_____

_____

_____

WHAT A COINCIDENCE!

"We need to be willing to let our intuition guide us, and then be willing to follow that guidance directly and fearlessly."
—Shakti Gawain

I pick up the phone to call my best friend, and she's already on the line. Or someone recommends a great book that inspired him, and the next day that same book falls right off the library shelf at my feet! Is this a coincidence? Yes! But it may be so much more than that.

Spirit speaks to me in many ways. Sometimes I think divine guidance comes through to me in these events that I call coincidences. God may be trying to tell me something that would inspire me or save me some real difficulty.

When coincidences happen, I like to think that they are divine reminders that God is right here with me and within me, loving me, guiding me, and protecting me.

I watch for divine signs, because the next coincidence I notice just might hold a special message of love and wisdom from God to me!

God's presence is at work in my life,
bringing me messages of love and wisdom.

Daily Word for Teens

TIME MANAGEMENT

◆

"Meditation creates more time than it takes."
—Peter McWilliams

With all the homework, family activities, sports, clubs, part-time jobs, and responsibilities around the house that might be on my calendar, I could use a personal assistant to help me keep on track!

Prayerful awareness is the key to managing my time. I invest a few minutes each day in prayer and in reviewing my schedule. This way, God and I are in charge of my life instead of my life being in charge of me. I keep a day planner of where I'm supposed to be and when, and I carry it with me. When I think of something I need to do, I write it in on the date that I need to do it. If it's a long-term project, I enter it on the date I need to start it and also on the date that it is due. I check my day planner regularly.

By looking over my schedule just after my daily prayer time, I am able to add a calm, peaceful focus to the upcoming day. I affirm every day that divine order is active in every event of my life.

Divine order is active in my life.
God and I are in charge!

VISION OF THE WORLD

———— ◆ ————

*"We look forward to the time when the Power of Love
will replace the Love of Power. Then will our world
know the blessings of peace."*
—William Ewart Gladstone

In school or on the job, I may let my mind wander at
times as I imagine how my life could unfold and what I'll
achieve. As the days go by and other possibilities occur to
me, my vision of the world never changes, however, for it
is always of a place of harmony and peace among all
people. This is a vision of how all the world can be blessed.

With willing hands and a loving heart, I ask God what I
can do to help make this vision a reality. The answer is:
Hold to this vision and live it as a reality every day of
your life.

Knowing that within me I hold the power to help
create peace adds enrichment and meaning to everything
I do. I am participating in a vision of harmony and peace
for the world that is becoming a reality more and more
each day.

*My vision of harmony and peace among all people
enriches everything I do.*

Daily Word for Teens

MY MISSION STATEMENT

—◆—

"Make your life a mission—not an intermission."
—Arnold Glasgow

Organizations often have mission statements that keep everyone pointed in the direction of a common purpose and goal. A good mission statement is short—just a few sentences—and easily remembered.

I, too, can write my own personal mission statement that keeps me moving toward my goals. To begin, I jot some ideas. I ask myself, What do I want to share with my world? Maybe it's expressing my thoughts as a writer, being a good listener, excelling in a sport, or sharing my talents through music.

Examples of mission statements are: *I dedicate myself to inspiring others by aiming for excellence as a figure skater; I am a student who is committed to doing my best; I devote my life to expressing the love and light of God to others.*

My mission statement can be specific or general. I can change it anytime my goals change. I keep it where I can see it, as a reminder of who I am and what is important to me.

I know who I am and what is important to me,
and I stay on the path toward my goals.

Daily Word for Teens

BEING MYSELF

◆

"Inside myself is a place where I live all alone and that's where you renew your springs that never dry up."
—*Pearl Buck*

Just being myself shouldn't be difficult. Yet there are times—especially when I am with someone new or in class or at a party—when I act differently than I usually would. In stressful times, why do I feel the need to pretend to be someone I'm not?

When I need help being myself, I pray:

"God, here I am in a situation in which I feel like a fish out of water. Help me to relax so that I can speak and act as the true creation of Yours that I am."

God helps me to know that it's okay to be me. That may mean I don't always say the brightest thing or act in the most graceful manner, but who does? I am not a programmed robot; I am a one-and-only me.

There is a lot of good within me just waiting for me to let it out. I can do this only by being myself and feeling comfortable with who I am. Expressing God's creativity when I speak and act comes naturally to me. I am simply being me.

By being myself, I release the good within me
that is waiting to be shared.

Daily Word for Teens

VACATION

◆

*"It is only when we silence the blaring sounds of our daily existence
that we can finally hear the whispers of truth that life reveals to
us, as it stands knocking on the doorsteps of our hearts."*
—K.T. Jong

Summer break is typically a time for family vacations.
As obligations and responsibilities change or increase,
however, family functions may take a backseat to a job,
sports, or summer classes.

But I don't need to get in a car or on a plane and travel
across many miles to feel the get-away-from-it-all sense
of freedom and rest that a vacation can give. At any time
of the day or night, I can mentally leave the homework or
the job behind and take a vacation.

To an onlooker, I may seem to be daydreaming or
simply spacing out, but what I am actually doing is
focusing my attention and energy within to the presence
of God that refreshes my mind, body, and soul.

In this quiet place within, I relax. Schedules, stress, and
concern don't exist here. Without going anywhere at all, I
have escaped to a place of rest and relaxation.

*I get away from it all and relax
by turning to the presence of God within.*

Daily Word for Teens

MEDITATION
Success

◆

Reaching an important goal inspires me to continue onward and motivates me to be successful in reaching other goals. Yet I don't want a seeming lack of success to keep me from setting and pursuing goals. So before I tackle any new project, I turn within to a quiet place. I pray to God for the inspiration and motivation I seek, and then I become still. When I pray, I am speaking to God, and when I meditate and still my thoughts, I am listening to God.

In these quiet moments, I relax and let the situations of the day slip away from me. Now that I have emptied my mind of all concerns, the peace of God quickly moves in to fill the void. I listen as God reassures me that I can succeed if I believe in and am willing to work toward what I want to achieve.

Renewed with inspiration and motivation, I continue on with my day, knowing that success is just around the corner.

I prepare to be successful by turning to God
in a time of prayer and meditation.

CAREER FOCUS

When I think about a career, I see myself working:
(check all that apply)

❏ with people
❏ with animals
❏ with numbers
❏ with ideas

❏ outdoors
❏ indoors

❏ at home
❏ in an office

❏ in one city
❏ traveling to many places

❏ by myself
❏ as part of a team

SOMETHING EVEN BETTER

BY KAT

I always had a weight problem—from kindergarten on. I remember the doctor telling my mom that my cholesterol was outrageously high for a child. But somehow I always found a way to get a supply of potato chips and candy, and then I would eat every bite.

My dad was in the military, and we moved from town to town, state to state, and even to other countries. From the time I was born until I went to college, we had moved nine times!

Being a military kid, I normally went to school with other children in the military. We knew that every few months someone would be leaving and someone new would be coming in. Never being in one place very long, I had to make new friends over and over again, and it was tough.

I also went through a phase where I had braces and wore glasses. Plus, I played the French horn, so it was hard to make friends even when I was on a bus full of kids. No one could sit next to me, because my French horn had to sit there!

I was probably more fortunate than others, though. I didn't feel lonely when I would go home, because I liked talking to my mom and dad. They would play board games with me, and my mother read to me in the evening when I was younger.

It wasn't until I got into eighth grade that I realized that, outside of the military, friendships could last longer than a few months. It was then that we moved to New Jersey and I attended my first civilian school. The kids there had known each other since kindergarten or first grade, and they all shared stories of past experiences that they had with one another. I started to feel like maybe I'd been a little ripped off with my childhood, and that bothered me. I even told my parents that I didn't want to move anymore. But eleven months later, my dad was transferred to Maryland and we moved once again.

My weight gain increased with each grade in school. By the time I enrolled in college, I weighed 205 pounds. I started taking acting classes and was able to work doing TV commercials. I was in demand because I resembled a famous talk-show host who also had a weight issue.

When I started to have severe backaches and to lose my hair, I went to see a doctor. I learned then that I had an endocrine disease called Polycystic Ovarian Syndrome. That put me in a tailspin, and I did a lot of soul searching, thinking *What have I done to my body?* I knew I didn't cause myself to have PCOS, but I sure hadn't done anything to help myself to be healthy. I was always careful to put a high grade of fuel in my car, but I had put junk food in the body that God had given me.

I prayed, "God, please help me lose weight!" All of a sudden I felt an answer to my prayer. It was as if God were saying to me: "Okay, here is the deal: If you eat right and exercise on a regular basis, I guarantee you that the weight will come off." I knew I could not have any better guarantee than one from God.

Surfing the Internet, I found so much helpful information about the importance of vitamins and plant-based nutrients. I read the labels on everything I ate—before I ate! In fourteen months, I had lost ninety pounds. I started getting calls from people who had heard that I had lost weight. I was hired as a correspondent for a fitness show and later worked on several other shows. Now I'm a health anchor for CNN Headline News.

When I was younger we had cable TV installed, and that was a big deal. Now I am a part of the entertainment industry—an industry that has grown: Satellite TV has hundreds of channels, and the Internet has billions of Web sites. Today we have even more sources of information streaming into our lives trying to sway our opinions. But I have something even better than all of these sources: I know that I can always look to God for help.

PROTECTED

———◆———

". . . The power of God protects me . . . "
—James Dillet Freeman

There is a simple but powerful prayer that comforts me whenever I feel lost or alone and calms me whenever I feel anxious or afraid. I say the *Prayer for Protection* silently or aloud at any time I need the reassurance of God's presence:

> The light of God surrounds me,
> The love of God enfolds me,
> The power of God protects me,
> The presence of God watches over me.
> Wherever I am, God is.

The light of God gives me wisdom, the love of God gives me comfort, the power of God gives me strength, and the presence of God gives me faith. Wherever I go, whatever I do, the spirit of God goes with me and also greets me at each destination. God's presence is within me, within all others, and within every particle of space on Earth and in the heavens. I am protected.

Wherever I am, God is with me,
loving and protecting me.

MATURITY

—◆—

*"Maturity begins to grow when you can sense your concern
for others outweighing your concern for yourself."
—John Macnaughton*

I know that maturity is not as much a matter of age as it is a matter of attitude. My own maturity comes with being aware of more than just myself and my needs and desires. It increases the more I care about the well-being of others and the conditions of the world. I don't stop with just being aware; I go ahead and do something to help other people and the environment.

I realize that my maturity comes with simple things, such as being on time and picking up after myself, and also with serious matters, such as driving a car with as much care when my parents are not with me as I do when they are.

Most of all, I think that maturity means allowing God's spirit within me to align my thoughts and words, my feelings and actions with what is for my good and the good of others. Then I am able to step outside my own little world into the big world.

*God's spirit within aligns my thoughts and words,
my feelings and actions with the goodness of God.*

Daily Word for Teens

GOOD JOB!

—◆—

"The reward of a thing well done
is to have done it."
—Ralph Waldo Emerson

With that sense of having done something worthwhile and having done it well, I am telling myself, "Good job!" I may have learned some new skill or was able to remain composed when someone lost his temper and was upset with me.

Raising my grade a point in math or science took time and a lot of dedication, but I did it! I didn't work hard just for the recognition of what I had done, but when someone acknowledged that I had done a good job, it helped!

I know joy in those moments when a feeling comes over me that God is telling me, "Well done." It really doesn't matter that no one else knows, for it is a message for me that I receive in my soul. I may not win first place in a race or a writing contest, but I have accomplished something by just participating. I have used my muscles—physical and mental—so that I am better off for doing what I did.

I know the joy of having done something worthwhile
and having done a good job.

Daily Word for Teens

FREE

*"I have memories—but only a fool
stores his past in the future."*
—David Gerrold

If I would allow it, negative events from the past could continually come to mind. They may be triggered when I see the people who were involved, when I hear a song that brings back a painful memory, or when I listen to someone else talk about a similar experience. But, thank God, I am free to choose not to allow those events to shape the present or the future.

The renewing spirit of God within frees me from the pain of the past. I cooperate with my own freedom by not reliving in memory whatever upset me last year or the year before. With the passage of time, I leave the past farther and farther behind.

I know that any feelings of uncertainty I may have are stirred up by my own thoughts. So it is up to me to free myself of limiting thoughts and feelings. I can by turning to God within for confidence, love, and peace of mind. I gratefully experience freedom of spirit, mind, and body.

Thank You, God, that I am free.

EXPECTATIONS

—◆—

"Sing to the Lord, bless his name. . . .
Declare his glory among the nations,
his marvelous works among all the peoples."
—Psalm 96:2–3

I know that the wisdom and love of God are blessing me every day. I receive greater blessings than I could ever have envisioned for myself. So rather than limit my good to only what I think I would like to receive or have happen in my life, I learn to expect unexpected blessings.

My expectations are no longer for a few particular things, but I expect and receive an abundance of blessings from God each day. With all walls that would limit my view knocked down, I look at the world around me with a sense of eager anticipation.

In true appreciation for the wonder of God that is everywhere, I am able to recognize that each and every person, animal, or natural wonder is someone or something unique that was created by the Master Creator.

With a sense of wonder and awe, I give thanks to God for unlimited blessings.

Thank You, God, for both expected
and unexpected blessings!

RESPONSIBILITY

—◆—

*"To decide, to be at the level of choice, is to take responsibility
for your life and to be in control of your life."*
—Abbie M. Dale

Showing up on time, doing my homework, and taking care of my chores at home are just a few of the ways that show how responsible I am. With integrity of character and action, I am able to answer for my conduct, and I am trustworthy. People can count on me because I am a responsible person.

This doesn't mean that one slip in being responsible negates a dozen times when I did act responsibly. My life and the lives of all people are God-given gifts. I have a reverence for life and a love for my Creator that encourage me to be responsible. This is not a heavy burden; it is a privilege that, when accepted and acted on, enriches my life with wonder and new adventures.

God has given me a life to live, and I am responsible for living it in a way in which the very qualities of love, wisdom, and compassion that God has given me show up in my daily life.

*Being responsible is a choice that I make and a privilege
that opens up a world of opportunity to me.*

MEDITATION
Time for Me

◆

I am so busy! My alarm clock goes off at an unbelievably early hour every weekday to remind me to get up and get ready for school. At school, the bell rings to remind me that it's time for class or lunch. When I get home, my parents nudge me to do my chores and my homework or get my clothes ready for the next day. These things are important, and many of them are for my own benefit, but that doesn't mean I always want to do them.

To keep a balance with my busy-ness, I consciously set aside small blocks of time for myself throughout the day. During these little breaks, I take a deep breath and let my mind be still. I check in with my feelings, blessing each emotion as I let it float on by. I feel my body becoming calmer. Then I turn my attention to God. I feel a sense of peace that increases the more I notice it. With just a few minutes of "me time," I am centered again in the peace of God.

In the midst of my activities,
I am centered in the peace of God.

FEARLESS

If I could get past the fear, what would I do
that I had been afraid to do before?

_____

_____

_____

_____

_____

_____

_____

_____

_____

_____

_____

GOOD ENOUGH

◆

"Nothing would be done at all if a man waited until he could do it so well that no one could find fault with it."
—Cardinal Newman

Writers, artists, and composers of music describe what they call a "block." Instead of a flow of creativity or an attitude of motivation, they sometimes become focused on negative self-talk: *This idea isn't interesting enough for a term paper; This painting will never be good enough for the art show; I'm not really talented.* Self-criticism and perfectionism can bring creativity to a screeching halt.

It's true that in math or science, there's often only one right way. But when it comes to most other pursuits, there are unlimited ways to express an idea, so there's really no such thing as "perfect." I approach my efforts with the attitude that they *are* good enough. I let my creative ideas flow with spontaneity and freedom, and then I work on improving them.

I smile when I realize that I, too, am God's creative expression in human form. I can improve, but I don't have to be perfect. I, too, am good enough!

*I am God's creative expression in human form,
and I am good enough as I am!*

Daily Word for Teens

RESPECT

*"Character is doing the right thing when nobody's looking.
There are too many people who think that the only thing
that's right is to get by, and the only thing that's wrong
is to get caught." —J.C. Watts*

I may have heard that respect for another person is
something that comes with time and understanding. Yet I
respect all people as God's creations, so I naturally respect
the basic right of all people to express their individuality
and to voice their opinions.

I treat others with kindness, rather than ridiculing them
if they dress or think or speak differently from me. By
doing this, I am showing respect for myself as well,
because no matter where I go, there I am. I can't run
away from anything I have said or done. I want to be able
to look at my own reflection in the mirror and feel a sense
of self-respect for the way I have treated others.

At all times God is gently guiding me in being loving,
so much so that being a loving person is a natural habit
for me. To everyone that I know currently or will meet in
the future, I show how much I respect all of God's
creations.

*As I show the respect for others that they deserve
as God's creations, my own self-respect grows.*

I Believe in Me!

---◆---

"I prefer to be true to myself, even at the hazard
of incurring the ridicule of others, rather than to be false,
and to incur my own abhorrence."
—Frederick Douglass

My self-esteem may take a blow if I make a mistake or
if somebody laughs at me rather than with me. Even if
someone does put me down, I won't stay down, because
I believe in myself.

I'm more than what people perceive me to be. I am
God's spirit expressed in a person. When others look at me
with more than a hint of doubt in their eyes or treat me as
though they are uncertain that I can handle something, I
look beyond the appearances they see. I continue to
believe in myself.

If I make a mistake, I am honest with myself and with
others. I admit what I did rather than try to blame it on
someone else. My self-esteem will not waiver, because I
know that I am constantly learning about myself and the
world around me. Besides, by taking responsibility for
myself, I am opening the door to any changes I may need
to make in myself or in the way I do things.

I am God's spirit in expression,
and I believe in myself.

TEAM PLAYER

◆

*"Individual commitment to a group effort—
that is what makes a team work, a company work,
a society work, a civilization work."*
—Vince Lombardi

I've heard it said that you can't win if you don't play, but I know the truth goes farther than that. Even if my team manages to win every game, I won't win as a person until I have mastered the skills of being a team player.

In basketball, team players pass the ball to others who might not be as good at making a basket, just so they can have a little practice and be included. Team players know that everyone in the group has strengths and weaknesses. Team players aren't out to show off their own abilities. They share their skills for the good of the team. They don't call attention to someone else's mistakes—instead they give encouragement and tips for how to improve.

On the team and in my life, I am a team player— someone who shines and lets others shine, acts in everyone's best interest, and promotes the whole team's success.

*I am a team player who encourages and inspires
everyone on the team to succeed.*

Daily Word for Teens

Almost There

◆

*"Wherever you go, no matter what the weather,
always bring your own sunshine."*
—Anthony J. D'Angelo

A positive attitude is one through which I look at a
glass and see it as half-full rather than half-empty. When
I think of the goals I have yet to reach, I see myself as
being almost there rather than thinking about how far I
have yet to go. Each day I do something that will take me
that much closer to what I hope to accomplish.

Making good grades and graduating from high school
are what I am aiming for. Each day, as I am attending
classes and studying, I am getting closer to realizing that
I am almost there!

Instead of feeling discouraged about how long it will
be before I'm out on my own, I consider the number of
days I have left as an opportunity to invest in myself and
in my future. This positive attitude helps me to see the
good in all things, including any seeming setbacks that I
may experience. So when I look at that glass, *yes,* it is
indeed half-full!

*My positive attitude is a great help to me
in meeting my goals.*

UNITY

"We are all in this together, by ourselves."
—Lily Tomlin

The strength in the unity of myself and my family and friends is greater than the sum of us as individuals. Like the single links in a chain, we create a strong bond that supports us as a unified whole.

So when I need some extra support in getting through a difficult time, I am not embarrassed to ask others to pray for me. I would do the same for them.

Our kinship and friendship unites us. Yet our unity survives those times when we don't get along and are all but ready to give up on one another. Our unity pulls us through, because we know that there is something beyond what we feel for one another. That something is our sacredness, which emanates from God's spirit within each of us.

The power of the universe unites us heart and soul through the fun times and the sad times. Nothing can separate or defeat us when we know that we are united in spirit with God and with one another.

Our individuality, kinship, and friendship with others are strengthened by our unity of Spirit.

Daily Word for Teens

MEDITATION
Here I Am, God

◆

My friends are important to me, and if one of them is going through a rough time and seems depressed and standoffish, I know that this could be his or her silent cry for help. But how do I know what to do or say to help?

God knows and God shows me as I close my eyes to outer appearances and open my mind and heart to receiving the right words of assurance. "Here I am, God. Lead me to what I need to do or say to be a source of love."

I immediately feel how comforting it is to be enfolded in the love of God. I feel at peace as I think about this same loving Presence there for my friend. Acknowledging the Creator's loving presence in my friend's life is a way that I can be of support.

Slowly opening my eyes, I give thanks that God is bringing comfort to my friends and me and that I can be of help by loving and praying for them.

God guides me in knowing how best to comfort and support my friends.

MAYBE I'LL SAY IT

These are the people I love who have never
heard me tell them, "I love you:"

_____

_____

_____

_____

_____

_____

_____

_____

_____

_____

_____

FIND YOUR HEARTSONG

BY MATTIE

My real name is Matthew, but I like being called Mattie. I home-school doing a high school curriculum. I began writing when I was about three years old, and now have a collection that contains thousands of poems, dozens of essays and short stories, and many illustrations.

I was born with a rare form of muscular dystrophy called mitochondrial myopathy. My sister, Katie, and brothers, Stevie and Jamie, had the disease, too, and all died in early childhood. My mom, Jeni, has the adult form of this type of muscular dystrophy, so we are both in power wheelchairs.

I also have dysautonomia; so I have a ventilator that breathes for me. I also need extra oxygen, monitors, and medicines. Getting out of bed is a chore. I put on my leg braces, take off my monitor . . . all kinds of stuff. Going to the hospital sometimes—that's a challenge. They poke and prod and do what people at hospitals do.

One way I cope with these challenges is writing poetry. Poetry is a great way of expressing your feelings in a way that you can understand them, and helps other people express their feelings and get through them, too. My friends and family always help me through a tough time with a hug or by saying "hi."

The most important factor in coping is my faith in God.

I feel that God is very close to me. My guardian angel, whoever that is, really toils hard.

I spent five months in a hospital this past year. My mother, Jeni, was encouraged to celebrate my eleventh birthday early, just in case I didn't live. Even though I had been in several comas, she waited. One time when I was almost unconscious, I saw angels coming to greet me. They were so beautiful I can't describe them by human concepts.

I celebrated my eleventh birthday in July with a party at the hospital. In August, the night before I left the hospital, Mom and I prayed that I would come home to live, not to die. The bleeding from my tracheotomy stopped.

For five years at summer camp, I made three wishes, releasing balloons for these intentions. First, I wished my poems would be published in books to help spread peace. While I was in the hospital, my first book, *Heartsongs*, was published, and my second book, *Journey through Heartsongs*, was published last fall. My hero, former President Jimmy Carter, wrote the introduction to *Journey*. My second wish was to talk about peace with Mr. Carter, and I was able to do that, too. My third wish was to meet Oprah Winfrey and share my message on her show. On October 19, Oprah and I read some of my heartsongs to her viewers. By November, both books were on the *New York Times* best-seller lists!

My books are about heartsongs. Your heartsong is your message, your inner beauty. It's what you feel you need to do when you are alive. Our heartsongs are beautiful. Every single one is different, and that's good.

Whether your heartsongs are about being a waitress or

becoming president, they are beautiful and in harmony. We need to be in harmony with our heartsongs.

After we are in harmony with our own heartsongs, we need to spread the peace. We need to stop fighting over little things, like land and money and religion. It doesn't matter how much land or money we have. It doesn't matter what we call God: "Buddha," "Allah," or "Yahweh." God is always one concept. There is something greater than we are. We just need to stop fighting and talk, and put together the beautiful mosaic of gifts that we are.

Prayer for a Journey

Thank You, God,
Not just for life,
But for our journey through life.
Life is a miracle,
And a journey through life
Is so full of so many more miracles,
If we travel with our Heartsongs.
Thank You, God,
For blessing me with the
Gift of Heartsongs,
So that I can enjoy my miracles.

ABOUT THE
DAILY WORD EDITORS

Colleen Zuck has been editor of *Daily Word* magazine since 1985. She also served as editor of *Wee Wisdom*, the longest continuously published magazine for children in the United States. Colleen is coauthor of *Daily Word: Love, Inspiration, and Guidance for Everyone; Daily Word Prayer Journal; Daily Word for Women; Daily Word for Families; Daily Word for Healing; Daily Word for Couples;* and *Daily Word for Weight Loss*. She lives with her husband, Bill, in rural Missouri.

Elaine Meyer has served in the Silent Unity ministry of Unity School of Christianity since 1987 and is the assistant editor of *Daily Word* magazine. In addition to being a published poet and photographer, she is coauthor of *Daily Word: Love, Inspiration, and Guidance for Everyone; Daily Word Prayer Journal; Daily Word for Women; Daily Word for Families; Daily Word for Healing; Daily Word for Couples;* and *Daily Word for Weight Loss*. Elaine, her husband, Dale, and their daughter, Caitlin, reside in rural Missouri.

Laurie Daven joined the *Daily Word* staff as associate editor in 2000 and also serves as a regional education consultant for the Youth of Unity, Unity's teen ministry. Since 1982, when she opened SnickerDoodle Studio in St. Louis, she has created over 150,000 caricatures and numerous editorial illustrations. She now resides in the Kansas City area.

If you would like someone to
pray with you—about anything at all—
you may call Silent Unity
24 hours a day
at (816) 969-2000.

◆

If you have no means of paying
for the call,
you may call (800) 669-7729,
or send your prayer request
by snail mail to:
Silent Unity
1901 NW Blue Parkway
Unity Village, MO 64065-0001
or online at:
www.unityworldhq.org